The Wood-carvers of Hong Kong

CRAFT PRODUCTION IN
THE WORLD CAPITALIST PERIPHERY

EUGENE COOPER

University of Southern California

WAVELAND
PRESS, INC.
Prospect Heights, Illinois

For information about this book, write or call:

Waveland Press, Inc.
P.O. Box 40
Prospect Heights, Illinois 60070
(312) 634-0081

G-ut 6/11

Cover photo: Courtesy of Sylvia Sensiper

Printed in the United States of America

7   6   5   4   3   2   1

CONTENTS

UNITS

The following are equivalents to units used in the text

LENGTH   AREA
1 foot = 0.3048 metres   1 acre = 0.405 hectares
1 inch = 0.0254 metres   1 mou = 0.61 hectares
1 li = 576.1 metres

                                  WEIGHT
                                  1 picul = 0.60 kilograms

MONEY
1 yen = £0.15 sterling (July 1973) = U.S.$0.39 (July 1973)
H.K.$1 = £0.077 sterling (July 1973) = U.S.$0.20 (July 1973)

ACKNOWLEDGEMENTS

It would be impossible to mention all the people who in one way or another contributed to the research effort which made this volume possible. First and foremost, I owe special thanks to Professor Morton H. Fried, the chairman of my dissertation committee at Columbia University, for his constant encouragement and unfailing support through the bleakest of times, and for his tolerance, open-mindedness and reassuring confidence in the value of the project from its very inception.

The other members of my dissertation committee, Professors Myron L. Cohen and Abraham Rosman of the Department of Anthropology, Professor Carl Riskin of the Department of Economics, Professor Andrew Nathan of the Department of Political Science provided valuable guidance and assistance both in the course of writing up the results of my research and in making valuable suggestions for the revision of the manuscript for publication.

Special thanks are due to the United States Office of Education under whose NDFL Title VI Fellowship my graduate coursework as well as a portion of the field research was pursued, and to the National Science Foundation whose Grant for Improving Dissertation Research in the Social Sciences quite literally made my field research possible.

It is fair to say that without the aid and advice of Mr Wang Tsun, Dr Marjorie Topley, and Dr James Hayes, my research could scarcely have got off the ground.

Mr Ng Moon-t'ong and Mr Ng Wah-leung deserve special mention for their tolerance, patience and willingness to share information about their trade with the ever present, ever inquisitive and occasionally bungling social anthropologist.

At key points in the course of the research, Mr Jimmy Chieh, Sir Douglas Clague, the officers and members of the Hong Kong Kowloon Woodwork Carvers Union, and Mr Cheung Ming-yu made important contributions that preserved the momentum of the research effort.

The staff of the Department of Anthropology at Columbia University, especially Ms Joyce Monges, deserve special thanks for their constant attention to my needs while in the field.

his willingness to listen, and to help me to thrash out ideas in the course of writing up the results of my research.

Finally I owe a special debt of thanks to my wife, Mrs Yuet-ling Cooper, who not only provided valuable guidance in the course of the research, supported the two of us during the write-up of the research results, put up with all the indignities associated with a resident Ph.D. candidate in the household, but also typed the final version of the manuscript in thesis form. Without her constant attention, good sense and good judgement during the past six years, it is fair to say none of the following would have been possible.

The conclusions and interpretations presented in this volume, however, are no one's responsibility but my own.

Hong Kong, 1978   Eugene Cooper

1

Introduction

This study documents the evolution of the mode of production of Chinese art-carved furniture and camphorwood chests, from its beginnings in late-nineteenth century inland peasant villages to its present-day elaboration in the British Crown Colony of Hong Kong. The data, both empirical and historical, justify the isolation of a middle period in that evolution, during which changes in the division of labor and class structure of craft production occurred. These changes in turn created the basis for the further development of a carved-furniture *industry* along capitalist lines, in the context of production for export in the world capitalist system.

I have chosen to describe the period in which such changes occur as a 'period of manufacture' (Marx 1967:1:336ff). Once the developments which characterize 'manufacture' are clearly understood, an otherwise seemingly unintelligible mass of data from a case study of craft production becomes a clear empirical demonstration of broad historical forces inherent in the evolution of the capitalist mode of production.

Before moving on to a discussion of the development of the art-carved furniture and camphorwood chests industry in China and later in Hong Kong, I should be a little more specific with respect to my use of terms, the phenomena I mean to isolate by use of those terms, and the theoretical and methodological implications of their use. This is all the more important since concepts like 'mode of production' are presently enjoying considerable vogue in the social sciences and, as is often the case with fashionable concepts, they tend to be used in a variety of ways.

The nub of the problem seems to lie in how to delimit the analytical scope of the concepts mode of production and social formation, which ultimately turns on the conceptual location of superstructural or ideological phenomena. On this latter question there is at present a disturbing lack of unanimity among neo-Marxist writers.

The concept of mode of production is generally taken to refer to a specific

1

combination of forces and relations of production. Forces of production refer to the actual means of production, their organization together with human labor power in productive activity, the state of productive technique within a given technological regime or at a given level of technological capacity. Relations of production refer to the way in which the means of production are owned and the social relations between men which result from their connections with the process of production (Dobb 1947:7). The relations of production define a specific mode of appropriation of surplus labor and a specific form of social distribution of the means of production (Hindess and Hirst 1975:9–10). The relations of production, in other words, determine the control and distribution of the factors of production as well as the output of productive activity.

Friedman (1972:9) uses the term mode of production to refer to the base or infrastructure of society, reserving the notion of social formation for a larger structure which combines infrastructure with juridico-political and ideological superstructure. This would seem to coincide with more or less accepted usage. However, both Friedman (1972) and Godelier (1972, 1977) have argued, in my view correctly, that no restrictions should be made regarding the kinds of elements which may take on infrastructural or superstructural functions, nor the number of functions which can be embodied in each element. Thus in precapitalist social formations, 'kinship structures may function as both relations of production and ideologies on which mythologies are constructed', and in capitalist formations 'juridical relations may merge with certain aspects of the relations of production as in capitalist property forms' (Friedman 1972:6).

Terray, however, has argued (1972:97, 179) that a mode of production is a three-part structure combining the economic base, juridico-political superstructure and an ideological superstructure. In adopting this approach, Terray follows Althusser in arguing that a social formation is the result of the 'combination of at least two distinct modes of production, one of which is dominant and the other subordinate' (Terray 1972:179).

A number of points arising from Terray's usage require comment. While I have accepted the idea that various social elements may function as both relations of production and ideologies, it would seem useful to keep these functions distinct, and to preserve the phrase mode of production for relations of the economic base. O'Laughlin (1975), in an otherwise comprehensive overview of Marxist approaches in anthropology, cannot seem to decide if a mode of production encompasses an associated superstructure (1975:358, 360), or whether superstructural phenomena are phenomena of the social formation (p. 367). I shall attempt to keep to the latter usage in which superstructural phenomena are relegated to the level of the social formation.

Terray's characterization of a social formation as consisting of several co-existing modes of production is quite useful. Godelier (1974:1), for example, also argues for the coexistence of multiple modes of production although he has criticized Terray, rightly in my view, for confusing the notion of mode of production in his own analysis with 'forms of capacity in social labor' and for inventing 'as many modes of production as there are labor processes' (Godelier 1977:24, 88).

Amin (1974b:57–8) also argues for the coexistence of multiple modes of production, but arbitrarily limits the possible number of modes of production to five: village commune, slave, tributary, simple commodity and capitalist. In a well-intentioned attempt to avoid the pitfalls of positing a dogmatic and mechanistic inevitability to history, Amin has also argued that apart from the village commune, to which he attributes historical priority, there is no necessary historical sequence to these modes. While such a position is quite laudable generally, it ought not to discourage inquiry into the processes by means of which modes of production come into existence and evolve.

For Amin, like Terray, historic societies are social formations 'characterized by a dominant mode of production which is interconnected with a complex set of other modes of production that are subordinate to it' (Amin 1974b:66–7). I would, however, agree with Godelier (1977:24), in contradistinction to Amin, that the nature and number of different modes of production which have been developed in history, or which may yet be found, solely or combined within any society, should not be prejudged.

Godelier has criticized some attempts to take the identification of new modes of production too far. He has justly criticized the notion of a lineage mode of production, 'supposed to designate "the" mode of production for most primitive societies with or without chiefdoms' (1977:87). He quite rightly argues that 'It is not [simply] by coupling Marx's concept of the "modes of production" to the concept of "lineage" that we can create "a new Marxist concept"' (1977: 88).

In this connection Sahlins' 'domestic mode of production' (Sahlins 1972: 41ff) could be criticized as constituting nothing more than a form of household level of socio-cultural integration, found as it is among the lowliest hunters and state-organized peasants. Since Chayanov's formulations regarding peasant household production and consumption are held by Sahlins to express the dynamic of the domestic mode (Sahlins 1972:102ff), despite the fact that Sahlins develops the concept in the context of tribes and chiefdoms, it seems clear that Steward's 'level of socio-cultural integration' (Steward 1955:43ff) more nearly describes the object of Sahlins' analysis than Marx's mode of production.

However, none of this should be taken as indicating that the search for new and as yet undescribed modes of production is a vain one. The nature and number of possible modes of production ought not to be determined *a priori*.

In the course of this volume, I shall be following the usage of Godelier as developed in his 'On the Definition of a Social Formation' (1974), in which a social formation is depicted as consisting of a number of modes of production

3

'which are found combined in a particular way within a specific society and *which constitute its economic base* at a specific period' (1974:63, emphasis added).

For Godelier, the analysis of a social formation requires the identification of the various elements in the social and ideological superstructure whose origin and function correspond to these various modes of production; the specification of the mechanisms by means of which the different modes are articulated and of the means by which one mode subjects the others to the needs and logic of its own reproduction; and lastly the spelling out of the manner in which the distinctive functions of each element of the superstructure, originating in the different modes of production, are recombined, redefined and given new content as they are subordinated to the demands of the dominant mode.

This scheme has the advantage of preserving the commonly accepted usage of mode of production as specifying relations of the economic base, while at the same time allowing for the coexistence of diverse elements within the economic base, each with its own associated superstructural elements. Analysis of the manner in which such elements are recombined, redefined and given new content in the course of the evolution of the Chinese art-carved furniture industry in post World War II Hong Kong constitutes an important aspect of this study (see especially Chapter 5).

I have already stated that I intend to trace the evolution of the mode of production of carved-wood furniture to its present elaboration in Hong Kong. There are good grounds for arguing that Hong Kong is really only a part of a larger Chinese social formation, if a somewhat aberrant part. The fact that the bulk of Hong Kong's food supply and much of its water is supplied by communes across the border in the Peoples' Republic; the fact that the Peoples' Republc earns the better part of its foreign exchange by marketing its manufactured goods in Hong Kong; the continuous flow of Chinese people back and forth across the border visiting relatives; the continuous flow of remittances sent to relatives in native villages on the mainland; the history of the treaty port experience in China of which Hong Kong is a direct product, all argue forcefully for the inclusion of Hong Kong in a larger Chinese social formation.

Nevertheless, more than 100 years of British rule, Hong Kong's thorough integration into the world market, its enormous sterling reserves and buoyant independent currency, its freest of free markets, and its unique post-1949 economic development could equally well support the argument that contemporary Hong Kong as a socio-economic unit ought to be treated as outside the pale of the present-day Chinese social formation.

It would seem to make the most sense to treat Hong Kong as a social formation of the British colonial 'periphery' in the sense in which Amin (1974a: 190) has used that term. In its externally oriented development, its disarticulated economy, characterized by marginal exchange and unevenness of productivity

4

between sectors, Hong Kong clearly manifests a number of important distinguishing characteristics of peripheral social formations described by Amin. It should, however, be noted that Hong Kong has made a virtue of this disarticulation, and has managed to create a distinctive niche for itself in the world capitalist system, in which it has been relatively successful in adapting to the demands of the international market (see Chapter 6).

It is not my purpose in this study, however, to analyze the Hong Kong social formation in its totality. Rather I shall be focusing on a single industry, analyzing the way in which its mode of production has *evolved*, first in the context of late nineteenth and early twentieth-century treaty ports, and later in the context of post-1949 Hong Kong.

This approach does not deny the coexistence of multiple modes of production in a given social formation, but is more concerned to discover the processes by means of which one of these modes of production is transformed and subordinated to the demands of a dominant mode, and seeks to specify precisely the steps by which that transformation is achieved. Although the social formation is not analyzed in its totality, this approach has the advantage of putting some empirical meat on the bones of the concept mode of production, a concept which some authors have maintained ought to remain highly abstract (see Amin 1974b:57), while at the same time making it more dynamic.

Thus, despite the disjointed character of economic development in the peripheral social formations of the world capitalist system as regards national economic integration, I shall argue that, at the level of the mode of production, the laws of capitalist development described by Marx for capitalism in the sixteenth to eighteenth-century European core of the world capitalist system quite adequately predict and explain the development of capitalist institutions in specified sectors of the present-day world capitalist periphery as well.

The notion of 'manufacture' is the case in point. The concept is one used by Marx to describe production in the period 'from the middle of the 16th to the last third of the 18th century' of European economic history (Marx 1967: 1:336). Manufacture typically arose in two ways. On the one hand it arose from the grouping together of formerly independent craftsmen into a single workshop to produce a single finished product. The archetypal example of this was carriage-making. The wheelwright, carpenter, upholsterer and blacksmith came together in a single enterprise to produce carriages, and gradually each came to lose the more generalized skills of his profession while specializing in the production of carriage parts. The formerly independent handicrafts 'become stripped of their independence and specialized to such an extent as to be reduced to mere supplementary partial processes in the production of one particular commodity' (Marx 1967:1:338).

On the other hand, manufacture arose from the progressive elaboration of the division of labor within a single craft, as occurred in Europe in pin-making. The process of production became increasingly broken-down into its various successive manual operations which came to be carried out simultaneously by a combination of detail laborers. In pin-making this meant the separation of wire drawing, pointing and heading into separate niches in the division of labor, each process being performed continuously by one or more detail laborers. Unit costs were thereby decreased, and productivity increased, in accordance with what has been called the 'Babbage principle'. A nineteenth-century political economist, Charles Babbage, pointed out that:

the master manufacturer by dividing the work to be executed into different processes, each requiring different degrees of skill or of force, can purchase exactly that precise quantity of both which is necessary for each process; whereas, if the whole work were executed by one workman, that person must possess sufficient skill to perform the most difficult, and sufficient strength to execute the most laborious, of the operations into which the art is divided (Babbage 1832:175–6 quoted in Braverman 1974:79–80).

In other words, 'the labor power capable of performing the process may be purchased more cheaply as dissociated elements than as a capacity integrated in a single worker' (Braverman 1974:79–80).

Although the division of labor is elaborated in the period of manufacture, each operation still 'has to be done by hand, retains the character of a handicraft, and is therefore dependent on the strength, skill, quickness and sureness of the individual workman in handling his tools. The handicraft continues to be the basis' (Marx 1967:1:338).

The Chinese art-carved furniture industry provides evidence of both processes characteristic of the rise of manufacture. Both the incorporation of formerly independent craftsmen into a single enterprise to produce a single finished product, *and* the elaboration of the division of labor of production, are manifest in its development (see pp. 12, 13).

In a regime of manufacture, the unity of the production process comes increasingly to reside in the capitalist who has brought the detail laborers together.

Hence the productive power resulting from the combination of laborers appears to be the productive power of capital . . . It is a result of the division of labor in manufacture, that the laborer is brought face to face with the intellectual potencies of the material process of production as the property of another and as a ruling power (Marx 1967:1:360–1).

It is in hand manufacture that the nature of capital as a social relation is realized, that the preconditions for the full development of capitalism are met. The producer becomes progressively divorced from the means of production (progressively proletarianized), and the means of production become increasingly concentrated in the hands of an emergent capitalist. We are not yet dealing with major technological change, although technological change may often occur as a climax in this process of primitive accumulation, but rather with changes in social relations. Marx is explicit on this point:

Cooperation based on division of labor, in other words, manufacture, commences as a spontaneous formation. So soon as it attains some consistence and extension, it becomes the recognized methodical and systematic form of capitalist production. History shows how the division of labor peculiar to manufacture . . . acquires the best adapted form at first by experience . . . and then . . . strives to hold fast that form when once found, and here and there succeeds in keeping it for centuries. Any alteration in this form, except in trivial matters, is solely owing to a revolution in the instruments of labor (Marx 1967:1:364).

In manufacture, the revolution in the mode of production begins with the labor power, in modern industry it begins with the instruments of labor (Marx 1967: 1:371).

Focus on hand manufacture hence emphasizes a two-stage process of industrialization, in which the historical contingency of future development shifts. It resides initially in the social relations of production, and only later do spontaneous rearrangements of that structure become the subject of greater technological possibilities. The transformations which characterize manufacture argue for the recognition that the relationship between the forces and relations of production cannot be specified *a priori*. It is rather in the interplay of the forces and relations of production that the course of historical development is determined.

This study, then, explores in detail the institutional structure of manufacture as it both explains and is in turn exemplified in the development of the Chinese art-carved furniture industry. When this exploration is completed, attention will be turned to the implications of the findings for theories of the nature and structure of social formations of the world capitalist periphery.

II

In pursuing this study, a variety of methodological tools were employed, ranging from a stint of intense participant observation to a survey of some 400 workers, factory bosses, shop owners and apprentices. In addition, I relied on a number of secondary sources which illuminate the subject of Chinese crafts, such as the pre-1949 work of such institutions as the Nankai Institute of Economics, the *Chinese Social and Political Science Review*, the *Chinese Economic Journal*, and such individuals as H. D. Fong, J. B. Tayler and Shih Kuo-heng.

Yet this study attaches particular importance to participation in actual production as necessary to a true understanding of economic phenomena in the real world. While recognizing that no observer leaves what he observes unchanged, this participatory methodology, rather than attempting to avoid the inevitable, enjoins the ethnographer to step directly into the behavior stream and to learn what he can about the structure of interpersonal relations by observing how that structure manifests itself in accommodating his presence. Such a methodology is in marked contrast to those in which the ethnographer attempts to withdraw from the behavior stream to observe its structure 'as if' he were not present.

The conviction that participation in production is necessary to a true understanding of economic phenomena is recognized in the institutional structure of the Peoples' Republic of China which requires periodic stints of production from its higher-level bureaucrats and cadres as a corrective for alienation from the effects of policy directives. In a trip to the National Minorities Institute in Peking in 1972 I had the opportunity to hear Professor Fei Hsiao-t'ung speak warmly of his experience at a May 7 cadre school where he learned to plant cotton (see Cooper 1973).* The inspiration for such institutional arrangements is firmly rooted in Maoist epistemology (see e.g. 'On Practice', Mao 1967:2: 295), which in turn has its roots in a concern of Marx's that as the division of labor became progressively elaborated in production,

the man of knowledge and the productive labourer came to be widely divided from each other, and knowledge, instead of remaining the handmaid of labour in the hand of the labourer to increase his productive powers . . . has everywhere arrayed itself against labour . . . systematically deluding and leading them (the labourers) astray in order to render their muscular powers entirely mechanical and obedient (Marx 1967:1:361, footnote in which Marx quotes W. Thompson, 'An Inquiry into the Principles of the Distribution of Wealth', 1824:274).

It is altogether fitting that a study of manufacture, in which the first steps in the elaboration of the division of labor of production occur, should reflect a concern on the part of the investigator to reunite the man of knowledge, the anthropologist, with the object of his knowledge, the laborers and the relations of production in which they interact. As a means to this end, I apprenticed myself as a wood-carver in a Chinese-run art-carved furniture factory as a base from which to pursue fieldwork. I was encouraged in this strategy by an active personal interest in artisanry, which made it possible for me to involve myself deeply in learning the basic techniques of the woodcarving trade.

My experiences as an apprentice put me on intimate terms with the daily routine of the factory. The relations of production and distribution of wood-carving factories and shops were soon very familiar to me. However, some information required a wider perspective than that obtainable on the floor of a single enterprise. For one thing, I had to assess the degree to which my experience of the carved-furniture industry at Heng Lung Co. was typical of the industry as a whole. There was, in fact, a great diversity in size, layout and organization of production units in the industry. I also required data on the

---

* A May 7 cadre school is a Chinese institution to which bureaucrats were often sent during the Cultural Revolution for stays of varying length for reschooling, retooling and education in the Marxist classics.

composition of the labor force and some of its distinctive features which could not be obtained at a single factory. Finally, no matter how deeply involved I was in production, there were some data which were impossible to come by. Access to the account books of Heng Lung Co., for example, was quite impossible.* Looking into the account books of any business is a delicate matter under any circumstances, and no amount of daily association with the work process, with my boss and his family in the course of my fieldwork, ever overcame his reluctance to sit down with me and go over the accounts of his business.

I was able to cover such gaps to a certain extent by administering the survey mentioned above, in the three months following my apprenticeship. During my apprenticeship I had come to know workers at some twenty-five to thirty carving factories through visits to other factories with my fellow workers. The high labor turnover (discussed on pp. 15, 62ff) meant that, during my apprenticeship, many of my fellow workers left Heng Lung Co. and went to work elsewhere, some even changing jobs two or three times during this period. By visiting them in their new sites of work I became acquainted with about half of the twenty-five to thirty factories mentioned. As my duties as an apprentice also included delivering finished goods to the shops that had ordered them, I was acquainted with several shop proprietors directly, and with many by hearsay. Finally, using a Merchants' Association† promotional pamphlet as a guide, I was able to locate about another twenty firms, despite the fact that the listings were hopelessly out of date.

Using all these contacts, a team, consisting of four students from the University of Hong Kong and Chinese University Hong Kong and myself, began the survey. We headed out to areas where we knew of at least one factory, and invariably found others of which we had no prior knowledge. This was especially so in the government resettlement factory blocks in North Kowloon and Hong Kong island, where large numbers of carved-furniture factories are concentrated. This enabled us to cover a larger number of factories than would otherwise have been possible. Questionnaires were administered to workers, bosses, and apprentices at their workplaces in the factories.

The seriousness with which most respondents took our work was gratifying. Hong Kong is not the kind of place in which one gives private information about one's life and economic circumstance to just anyone who comes in off the street and asks. Furthermore, none surpasses the Chinese wood-worker in talent for

---

* It was only when I returned to Hong Kong five years later, as a lecturer at the University of Hong Kong, that, after much coaxing and cajoling I was finally given the opportunity of going over the by then dusty old accounts of Heng Lung Co. for the period of my fieldwork, with my boss's son. For this I am deeply grateful. However, rather than simply verifying my own reconstructions and estimates of Heng Lung Co.'s business, the account books introduced some interesting ambiguities that required further analysis (see Chapter 6).
† Hong Kong Kowloon Art-Carved Furniture and Camphorwood Chests Merchants' Association — see Chapter 7.

playful deceit. Nevertheless, the survey showed most respondents willing to cooperate with our venture for the twenty minutes necessary to administer a questionnaire, and sometimes a good deal longer.

Most respondents were careful in their responses, and many even guarded. Refusals to reply to particular questions were accepted and the balance of the interview was conducted without pursuing such matters further. This resulted in a highly divergent number of responses for each question.* However, it is my belief that, for the most part, where information was given it was given frankly.

The results made it possible to assess the degree to which crafts continue to run in families, and to estimate roughly the composition of the workforce as regards place of origin, attitudes and preferences for certain conditions of work, and the extent of labor mobility. I was also able to gather a certain amount of statistical data of a general nature about business practices, percentage composition of business expenses and business conditions in general.

In addition to providing data on the history of the industry, the survey helped to put my experiences as an apprentice in larger perspective, in many cases verifying those experiences, in certain cases inspiring revision of impressions gained in those experiences, in other cases providing the gateway to whole new areas of thought.

III

The modern Hong Kong art-carved furniture and camphorwood chests manufacturing industry developed out of a peasant side-occupation; an essentially architecturally-oriented wood-carving (carving in relief) with which local temples in central China were often decorated, and the techniques and motifs of which had existed since T'ang times (A.D. 618–906) (Stanley 1914:78).

Chinese-style furniture had begun to be imported to Europe in the eighteenth century, primarily from Canton, which was the designated port of trade of the Chinese empire before the Opium War. Ship captains of the British East India Company contracted with the Co-hong merchants for articles of furniture in western as well as Chinese styles, which found their way back to Europe in the eighteenth and nineteenth centuries. The trade remained bureaucratically controlled by the Co-hong merchants who possessed an imperially mandated monopoly in overseas trade, of which furniture was but one item. This monopoly was broken in 1842 when the British, in the Opium War, demanded and won the right to deal with China according to Britain's *laissez-faire* principles of overseas trade.

1754 had marked the publication in England of Sir Thomas Chippendale's *The Gentleman and Cabinet Maker's Directory*, 'being a large collection of the most elegant and useful designs of household furniture in the Gothic, *Chinese*,

* The number (n) of respondents who gave information for each question referred to in the text is shown in parentheses ($n = x, y, z$).

10

and Modern taste' (Ferguson 1939:111, emphasis added). Chippendale himself was known to have executed many pieces after Chinese design, although it was a pattern which he rather quickly abandoned.

An overseas market for Chinese furniture had, however, been established. This Canton-centred trade was primarily in rosewoods (the Chinese *hua li* and *xuan zhi*) most of which had to be imported to the empire from southeast Asia, to which Canton was near. The factory in which this study was carried out had its immediate origins in a teak and camphorwood trade focused in Shanghai, after that port had been opened by force of English arms in the Opium War. There were no longer any bureaucratic fetters present in this period. He who could produce fastest and cheapest made the most money. The furniture industry had been incorporated into the world capitalist system. By 1876 Chinese furniture manufacturers had already participated in the United States International Exhibition in Philadelphia, where much of their merchandise was displayed, and presumably sold (Crossman 1972:185, Pl. 155).

The modes of production organization which evolved in this period of free trade in both Canton and Shanghai had begun to converge and when their practitioners scrambled out to Hong Kong to continue trading in a free market setting after 1949, two very similar structures of production combined to launch both the rosewood and teakwood trades in Hong Kong. While the distinction between these trades was preserved to a certain extent in the early post-1949 period by the persistence of largely discrete labor forces in rosewood and teakwood production, this distinction has today all but disappeared.

As larger numbers of foreigners became resident in Chinese treaty ports following the Treaty of Shiminoseki in 1895 that concluded the Sino-Japanese War, a style of furniture came into being which derived from the use of Chinese art objects and decorations in European-style furnishings. Carved woodwork, such as appeared on temples and shop fronts as independent ornamentation, and within such traditional furniture items of the wealthy as the so-called 'Ningpo beds', began to be incorporated into newly made furniture, designed and colored to be distinctly oriental, yet suited to western needs (Sowerby 1926:2).

Original temple carvings, so highly valued by furniture makers catering to this new western craze, were soon in short supply and some looting of temples to secure such carvings is known to have occurred (Sowerby 1926:2). Evidence from 1926 indicates that furniture manufacturers in the treaty ports had already begun placing orders with rural temple carvers for carvings of their own specifications. This not only insured a supply of adequate carvings, allowing the manufacturer greater command over the design of the finished product, but also increased employment opportunities for temple carvers (and carpenters) in the rural hinterlands of Shanghai.

According to older workers in today's industry, this stage in the development of the industry was grounded in a putting-out system, with its focus in Shanghai furniture factories and its outworkers in the small villages of Zhejiang province, in counties like Dongyang, Jinhua and Shaoxing. An agent from Shanghai would distribute raw materials to carpenters and carvers in their homes and would return at intervals to collect the finished work. Brought back to Shanghai, these carvings were incorporated into the furniture which began to find a wider market overseas, particularly among Americans.

The putting-out structure of the industry survived in Zhejiang till the revolution of 1949, but the expansion of the overseas market had by 1949 already led to the intensification of demand along the lines of this putting-out framework. In some cases, this led to the grouping of wood-carvers under one roof with carpenters and painters in urban Shanghai furniture factories.

Similar developments had accompanied the opening of export markets for other Chinese crafts. Theodore Herman has demonstrated how the 'pull of the market' led to the creation of coastal craft industries such as carpet, pottery and jade industries in Chinese treaty ports, and how, because of their easier access to overseas buyers and sometimes materials, these coastal industries soon overshadowed the inland crafts that spawned them (Herman 1954:29).

For the carved-wood furniture industry centered around Shanghai, these developments never ran their full course, as socialist revolution intervened. The full blossoming of hand manufacture, heralded as it was by the incorporation of several separate craftsmen under one roof in Shanghai in a carved-furniture industry, had to await the industry's post-revolution relocation in Hong Kong.

In the post-1949 period, the communist government tried to reverse the movement of the carved-furniture industry toward Shanghai back into the rural counties. Rural Dongyang county now sports a complete furniture manufacturing industry of some 1,000 workers centered in the county itself.

It can therefore be assumed that trade in the industry was disrupted in the early post-revolutionary period. The large number of refugees, furniture workers and factory owners, Cantonese as well as Shanghainese, who made their way to Hong Kong at this time is also evidence of this. However, it should be pointed out that several of the factory owners who moved their businesses to Hong Kong maintained portions of their businesses in Shanghai until as late as 1953. Many undoubtedly hoped that, socialist revolution or no, the government might encourage native businesses to remain open; others perhaps hoped for a Nationalist counter-attack that would restore a more favorable business atmosphere.

When it became obvious that this latter condition would not materialize out of the Korean War, and that the former could never come to pass as the United States put a trade embargo on all goods of Communist Chinese manufacture in the period after the Korean War, those who had stayed in the hope of revitalized business soon found their way to Hong Kong as others had somewhat earlier. The United States constituted the largest market for carved-wood items which the industry produced. An embargo meant that the trade was best pursued elsewhere than in Communist China.

The trade embargo was a boon to the newly relocated factory owners in the wood-carving trade in still British-controlled Hong Kong. It gave them, as a group, a virtual monopoly of the largest market for Chinese carved-wood products. It was this relatively enormous market which governed the entire Hong Kong based development of Chinese-made carved-wood furniture, and even led to the introduction of the industry to Taiwan somewhat later, where carved teakwood furniture had never been produced indigenously to any large extent. It provided a setting in which accumulation of capital could occur unimpeded by any restrictions, except that of competition between producing units in Hong Kong.

The appeal of the finished commodities of the industry was their craft, that is, their carved, nature and they were therefore not subject to competition from any western mass-produced substitutes. These conditions made it possible for the factory owners to consolidate in Hong Kong the institutional transformation by means of which a regime of manufacture had been achieved in Shanghai and Canton, and to launch on its shoulders, as it were, the development of a modern furniture industry.

The organization of production adopted at that time was based on the earlier models, and the size of the market led to an enormous proliferation of these manufacturing units, large and small, which still operated without machinery, but in which a suitable division of craft labor was established.

Each unit consisted of a group of carvers, carpenters and painters. The carvers, in a manner characteristic of the division of labor in hand manufacture were subdivided into two types — rough- and smooth-carvers. The rough-carvers blocked out the basic design of the carving, organizing the figures and the motifs and their composition, establishing the appropriate proportions, etc. (see Plate 1). The piece was then passed to the smooth-carver to smooth out the rough edges, concentrate on the detail and line work and finish with care the faces of the characters (see Plate 2), while the rough-carver began a second piece. From the smooth-carver, the finished pieces (see Plate 3) passed on to the carpenters in the factory, who incorporated the finished panels onto the frame which they had in the meantime been preparing and the item of furniture was thus completed. Often the furniture was shipped out to a retailer in the raw and only stained and varnished in the rear of the retail outlet in the tourist section of Kowloon, but just as often a factory maintained one or several painters on hand to finish the goods on the factory site (see Chapter 3).

All production units maintained roughly the same proportions of practitioners in each stage of the production process throughout the 1950s. Factory owners with larger capital assets hired larger numbers of workers, but the proportions were roughly maintained.

Throughout this period, the proliferation of production units which occurred

The wood-carvers of Hong Kong

1. The process of rough-carving

2. The process of smooth-carving

3. A finished carving

to meet the demand of the American market led to an increasing demand for skilled labor in the industry. Large numbers of Cantonese workers whose families had never before worked in the industry, or whose families were engaged in the Canton-centered rosewood industry, were either taken on as apprentices or, where they had the means, began their own carved-teak establishments.

The demand for labor and the breadth of the market made it impossible for the refugees from Zhejiang and Shanghai to impose a monopoly on jobs in the teakwood industry for members of their own group. While they still maintain a sort of aristocracy in the labor force as regards their purported superior carving and carpentry skill in teak, they have for more than twenty years been working side by side with Cantonese fellow workers, or for Cantonese bosses, and the recruitment base of the labor force has broadened.

The shortages of labor in this period had other consequences. It meant that in a free market for labor which the British Colonial government strove to maintain, workers in the carved-wood products industry were in an advantageous position in setting the terms of their employment. The rather high mobility rate between firms in the same industry today may well be projected back to the 1950s. Where workers had little protection or security in employment, they took advantage of labor scarcity to sell their skilled labor to the highest bidder.

The wood-carvers of Hong Kong

It is not unusual today to find workers changing jobs from month to month for slightly higher rates of pay.

Thus throughout the 1950s the industry retained its craft basis and skilled workers were its cornerstone. Skilled workers are always difficult for capital to deal with, particularly so in a regime of hand manufacture where 'the mechanism of manufacture as a whole possesses no framework apart from the laborers themselves' (Marx 1967:1:367). That this was so in the early Hong Kong based art-carved furniture industry is shown by the fact that, of a total of seventy-five factory and shop bosses questioned about the factors most important to success in the industry, a third (twenty-six) mentioned maintaining good relations with workers; this was by far the most frequent response.

In this context, workers were able to maintain a number of privileges which characterized an earlier era of less expansive production and accumulation, and which came to afford them some protection from market forces, whose impersonal operation increasingly determined the level of their wages. Today one can still find factories in which workers eat with the boss and his family and often sleep in the factory. The boss, by providing these extras, attempts to insure his supply of scarce labor. However, many bosses have long since given up trying to deal with workers so delicately, particularly since their efforts were often wasted on unappreciative skilled workers whose labor was in such demand. Workers' loyalty to the firm had to be bought at a high price under such conditions.

In spite of this, business conditions remained favorable to capital throughout the 1950s as is revealed in the following figures. By 1958, wooden furniture exports totalled H.K.$10.1 million and by 1960 they peaked at H.K.$18.1 million. Camphorwood chests exports followed a similar pattern peaking in 1960 at H.K.$1.64 million (Ruscoe 1963).

1960 marked the highpoint and also the beginning of the end of the manufacturing period, in the development of the art-carved furniture industry. Export figures for carved-wood items *per se*, as represented by figures for camphorwood chests, only broke through the H.K.$1.64 million mark again thirteen years later, when overall output of carved chests dropped more than 40% in two years. The increase in value of exports for 1973 clearly reflected a steep rise in prices rather than any expansion in production.

It was also in 1960 that labor organizations, which had come into existence in the early 1950s, began to demand a larger share in the prosperity of the industry, which still operated in a division of labor characteristic of manufacture. Three unions had come into being in the teakwood and camphorwood line of furniture manufacture in the early 1950s — two of carvers, the other of carpenters.* Workers in the separate crafts out of which the industry had developed

---

* A union of carvers and carpenters in the Canton-based rosewood industries had been created in 1922, when Sun Yat-sen was involved in the organization of workers around Canton the better to secure their livelihood. His Guomindang party was still allied with the

thus gave social expression to the manufacturing division of labor in the form of titularly separate unions of carvers and carpenters. Ch'en Ta, a noted Chinese social scientist, has shown how, in certain Chinese industries of the 1920s, this craft parochialism led to difficulty in pressing the unified demands of an emergent industrial proletariat (Burgess 1928:223–4).

As in the 1920s, the situation in post-1949 Hong Kong was further complicated because the independent craft unions came to serve as the basis for the expression of the differing political views of the workers. One so-called 'carvers' union' owed allegiance to the mainland Chinese Communist government, and soon became the labor organization of all workers of communist persuasion — carvers, carpenters and painters. The 'carpenters' union' which owed allegiance to Chiang Kai-shek and his Nationalist government became the labor organization for all workers of nationalist persuasion.*

The strike which occurred in 1960 hence reflected not only a demand for an increased share of the profits of a prosperous industry, but also a contest between unions of competing political affiliation to win greater gains for their constituents, so that each could thereby prove the superiority of its political stripe. A kind of one-upmanship operated during the dispute in which the numerically inferior forces of the nationalist unions succeeded in winning a raise of 22% for their members, while the numerically larger forces of the communist union settled earlier for a 20% increase.

Thus in 1960, a division of the labor force which was bequeathed to the industry under hand manufacture became the vehicle for the expression of political ideologies more characteristic of a capitalist mode of production.

Within the year a merchants' association was organized as the bargaining agent for the bosses, and labor and capital faced off as organized antagonists. The merchants' association was able in the next series of labor disputes to use the political divisions of its labor force to its own best advantage.

Out of the period of prosperity which reached a climax in 1960 came the real source of the ultimate decline of 'manufacture', in the sense in which I have used that word. Power-driven machinery was introduced into the carpentry stage of production. This changed the established ratio of carvers to carpenters required in a given production unit. The introduction may have been the result of the fact that the construction industry in Hong Kong was booming by the mid-1960s, and large numbers of carpenters were being wooed away from the furniture industry by higher wages in construction. This may have created a serious shortage of carpenters which provided the impetus for the adoption of

Chinese Communist party at that time. The rosewood union is still operating in Hong Kong today although it is of only marginal concern (See Chapter 5).

---

* An independent union of Shanghai and Zhejiang carvers of nationalist persuasion was formed in 1960. Although it does not seem to have been involved in the 1960 dispute, it surfaced in a dispute in 1964, and seems to have passed out of existence since then (see Chapter 5).

power-driven machinery.* In any case, it may very well have been the construction industry which made available the new machinery by means of which the carpentry stage of the production process was revolutionized.

Once these new devices were adopted, probably at first by the larger manufacturers, such as George Zee, J.L. George and Far Eastern Furnishings (all firms of Shanghai/Zhejiang capital), it became imperative for the smaller firms to follow suit, and increasingly large amounts of capital were soon required to run a business in the industry effectively.

The increasing capital intensiveness of the industry in its carpentry stage, while not fully undermining the craft basis of the industry, which still persisted in the hand-carved portions of the furniture produced, nevertheless compelled the factory owners to seek a wider market for their goods.

The market for carved-wood products, if camphorwood chests can be taken as an indicator, was fairly well saturated. By 1971, exports had still not surpassed the H.K.$1.64 million mark set in 1960, and by 1971 Australia rather than the United States accounted for 50% of the sales of only H.K.$1.46 million. Export figures for 1973 and 1974 stood at almost H.K.$1.80 and H.K.$1.69 million respectively but, as mentioned above, overall output declined substantially in both these years, and figures for 1975—7 fell substantially below the H.K.$1.64 million mark once again.

Concentration of capital and saturated markets made diversification the watchword of the day. This strategy is being implemented today by the sons of bosses of some of the larger factories in town. Having returned from the United States and Canada with degrees in Business Administration, a few have taken over the old family businesses and injected them with modern accounting procedures, permanent office staffs, plans for streamlining the apprenticeship system, and a knowledge of the requirements of overseas markets that leave their old fathers dumbfounded. They have encouraged greater production of modern-style furniture − sofas, tables and chairs − in the more elaborated division of labor which power-driven machinery permits, although their shops in the tourist section still boast a few carved showpieces.

But they are after much more than the curio market in which carved camphorwood chests had their heyday, and several will do consignments for luxury department stores in the United States and Japan. Large numbers of companies are coming to market their goods independently rather than through retail outlets or through commercially oriented middlemen.

These latter had, in Republican times (1911—49), provided the small producer of Chinese crafts with access to the overseas market, when and wherever such a market existed, and they did so for a profit. Herman describes such a class of middlemen as dealing in many commodities. When it served their interests (for example when the demand fell off) they were able to absorb their losses in a

* The fact that it was not the machinery that displaced the carpenters is evidenced by testimony from factory owners who lived through the period.

18

single commodity by cancelling orders and leaving the manufacturer to bear the loss (Herman 1954:182). The life of the craft manufacturer in the Chinese treaty ports was precarious at best.

In the Hong Kong based art-carved furniture industry, the manufacturer had the option of dealing with local retailers who did a thriving business with tourists and many of whom had at one time or another owned their own furniture factories. Some of these retailers even shared the same place of origin with the manufacturer. In any event, the post-war market for Hong Kong carved-wood furniture was large enough to guarantee that the demand would not dry up, and this reduced the significance of the middlemen as a class to the manufacturer.

Today, larger capital requirements, widening and diversified markets and greater business sophistication bring independent marketing within the capability of a larger proportion of actual production units. More importantly, a wider market has been found to absorb the now more diverse commodities of the Hong Kong furniture industry.

By 1968, the exports of Hong Kong made wooden furniture had climbed to more than H.K.$25 million, and by 1971 had jumped to nearly H.K.$44 million. By 1974 wooden furniture exports peaked at almost H.K.$83 million and, after a small decline in 1975, shot up to more than H.K.$122 million in 1977 (Hong Kong Productivity Council 1972; Hong Kong Trade Statistics 1972–7).

Carved-wood products represent a progressively decreasing percentage of those figures, and this may indicate a further undermining of the craft basis of the industry. The significance of the craft nature of the product has declined as a feature of its marketability. The carver has begun to lose his importance to the industry as a whole.

Not surprisingly, the quality of carving in Hong Kong made carved-wood furniture is declining. The most highly skilled carvers push their sons into carpentry or into business rather than teach them a 'useless' dead-end occupation like carving (see Chapter 8). Anyone interested in purchasing carved-wood furniture or camphorwood chests with really impressive carved portions, is well advised to spend a little more money and purchase products of Mainland Chinese manufacture. There production has not yet become so highly intensified, but may become more so as China seeks to increase its luxury exports to earn foreign exchange.

Carpentry, meanwhile, has become increasingly automated in Hong Kong. Marx (1967), Bücher (1901) and Polanyi (1944) have all noted in one way or another that modern industry (as opposed to manufacture) makes man the tender and hence extension of a machine, by taking out of his hands the tool which was an extension of himself. This process of more thorough alienation from the means of production began in the Chinese furniture industry in carpentry in the 1960s, but is only running its course today in the largest furniture factories in Hong Kong, such as Far Eastern Furnishings and Cathay Furniture. By early 1974, carpenters were becoming increasingly specialized into drill press operators, sawyers, assemblers, etc. Power-driven machinery had provided the means of breaking down the division of labor which characterized the manufacturing period even further. The nature of work had begun to change. A new mode of production was emerging.

Organized labor will have a large voice in determining the manner in which that mode of production evolves, particularly the numerically dominant and today more vital left-wing 'carvers' union'. While they may not be able to prevent the deterioration of the carvers' position in the industry, they can perhaps preserve among their carpenter members the all-round skill which they until recently required. At the moment, although the tools of production have passed out of their member-carpenters' hands, the union is well disposed to fight to maintain the preponderant influence of skilled labor in the industry, against the tendency for specialization to cheapen their members' labor power.

Skilled workers are still predominant in the industry. They are as hard to control on the job as ever, and they are still selling their labor in a seller's market. The union has taken advantage of the now legitimate position of the Peoples' Republic of China as representative of the Chinese people in the United Nations, to which its members owe allegiance, to mount a serious and sustained recruitment drive, winning a host of new members among workers in the industry. Armed with the thought of Chairman Mao, the union can bring to bear the not inconsiderable institutional leverage which his thought affords in Hong Kong (such as the resources of the Hong Kong Federation of Trade Unions and ultimately the resources of the Peoples' Republic itself).

Their principal adversary in shaping the new mode of production is the now all-but-dormant Merchants' Association, whose success in the confrontations to come will depend on its revitalizing itself as an organization of big capital, capable of dealing with the highly organized workers on more equal terms. This had not occurred in 1974. At that time the Merchants' Association could only be characterized as an organization of small manufacturers, a social survival of a time when the predominant productive unit was much smaller.

If it does revitalize, the Merchants' Association must win over the support of the larger, more highly capitalized firms in the industry. The Association's current membership could not even muster a fight in 1973 when they were forced to grant the left-wing union a 25% increase in wages. If labor continues to wield such power in the industry, it could drive all but the largest manufacturers out of business by increasing the production costs of the small enterprise precipitously. The only other option open to the small manufacturer is to reorganize his business and increase his outlay for capital equipment. This option also makes an anachronism of the smaller manufacturer and his old Merchants' Association.

The details of the mode of production of Chinese art-carved furniture as a modern industry will be determined in the process of resolution of the future confrontations between organized labor and capital, whether the latter is organized or not. Whatever institutional developments do occur will be firmly rooted in the institutions that arose during the period of manufacture, many of which still remain, many of which have changed or begun the process of change to meet new requirements, and some of which will undoubtedly resist change.

What has been said so far provides the categories in which this investigation of the modern Hong Kong art-carved furniture industry was pursued.

Chapter 2 examines the institution of apprenticeship in the art-carved furniture industry and its role as a strategic institution in the struggle between labor and capital for control of the quantity, quality and value of labor power as the industry evolved through hand manufacture.

Chapter 3 deals in greater detail with the organization and relations of production in the industry and analyzes how the organizational requirements of furniture production changed from early 'manufacture' to present-day industrial production. Social relations centering on the workplace are analyzed in this context.

Chapter 4 discusses workforce composition, social divisions and other work-force features as they developed in the context of the skilled-labour scarcity that has prevailed in the art-carved furniture industry in its manufacturing and modern industrial phases. Findings are compared with what is known of such factors in the Republican Chinese setting.

Chapter 5 addresses the phenomenon of trade unionism in the art-carved furniture industry; how it developed in a context of traditional craft parochialism and how it finally overcame those constraints as the mode of production of carved-wood furniture developed and changed. The activities of the dominant communist-affiliated Hong Kong Kowloon Woodwork Carvers' Union, and its conscious adaptation of traditional Chinese institutional forms in a manner consistent with an ever more appropriate proletarian ideology, are examined in detail.

Chapter 6 examines commercial relations and the structure they generate within Hong Kong society. The commercial activity of Heng Lung Co. and its business practices are described and analyzed.

Chapter 7 deals with the Merchants' Association, its past activity and current inactivity in pursuit of the interests of its member firms. Its role as a repository of traditional ceremonial reverence of the craft founder, Luban, and its other organizational continuities and discontinuities with traditional Chinese guilds are discussed.

Chapter 8 is a biographical and ideological sketch of one of Hong Kong's exceptionally skilled carvers, and discusses the craftsman's relation to his work and how it has changed in the context of growing capital accumulation and market diversification.

21

The wood-carvers of Hong Kong

Chapter 9 returns to the concept 'manufacture' and explores some of its wider theoretical and practical applications for the study of modes of production and social formations of the world capitalist periphery.

2

Apprenticeship

This chapter seeks to analyze the ways in which apprenticeship in the production of Chinese art-carved furniture and camphorwood chests has changed as the mode of production evolved through a regime of craft 'manufacture' toward industrial capitalism. Apprenticeship, as the institutionalized means of labor force reproduction, governs both the quantity and quality of labor power reproduced by establishing the rate at which new workers are turned out and the content of their training. Ultimately, as a result of both these factors, apprenticeship also governs the value of the labor power reproduced, and thereby determines the wage it can command in a free labor market. It has therefore been a strategic institution in the struggle between labor and capital for control of the quantity, quality and value of labor power as the institutions of craft production have developed and changed.

The traditional exclusiveness of Chinese craft occupations is well documented (see Gamble 1921, MacGowan 1888). Associations of craftsmen (guilds) restricted in every way they could the number of practitioners operating in a trade. It was part of the common interest of all practitioners to enforce an oligopoly, and craftsmen seldom allowed their skills to be taught widely outside their extended families (see Hsü and Ho 1945). The generic relation between guilds and castes has been noted by Childe (1950:7), and Marx, for example, has written:

Castes and guilds arise from the action of the same natural law that regulates the differentiation of plants and animals into species and varieties, except that when a certain degree of development has been reached, the heredity of castes and the exclusiveness of guilds are ordained as the law of society (Marx 1967: 1:340).

Among the most important means of enforcing this exclusiveness was a rigorous apprenticeship ordeal, which not only further insulated the skills of the craft from outsiders, but required a firm determination on the part of even a craftsman's kin to gain entry into the relatively privileged ranks of the skilled artisan.

The lot of the Chinese apprentice was never a pleasant one. He was a veritable prisoner, bound to his master by contract, underwritten by a guarantor, usually for three years and three months (three years and a festival), sometimes longer.

During this contract period, the boy is entirely under the control of his master. He is in fact bound hand and foot. Even in cases of sickness and death the boy has no claim against his master, and the expenses of any care may be charged up to the head of the family or the guarantor (Ch'u and Blaisdell 1924: 31).

Should the apprentice fail to fulfill the contract, the guarantor was usually required to reimburse the master for the money paid out in food and clothing during the first year before the apprentice had supposedly begun to earn his own keep. Since such expenses were usually well beyond the means of the apprentice or his family, conformity to the master's wishes was imperative for the duration of the contract.

The demands made upon the apprentice were considerable. He led a Cinderella-like existence in which he was

the footman of the store. All members above the apprentice are entitled to ask him to do errands for them. Cleaning the toilet, preparing the tea, working on piles of laundry are other forms of his assignment. Anything done not to the satisfaction of the members and especially the *laopan* [the boss] is surely rewarded by spanking, kicking or beating . . . He never has a bed of his own; he moves around making use of benches and tables, spreading whatever bedding he may possess on them . . . His life is a soldier's life at the front; instead of facing gun powder, he is in constant threat of punishment. He learns how to endure. He eats too, only after everybody else has finished eating. What is left on the plate is what belongs to him − the old miscellaneous odds and ends. It is little wonder that we find most of them underfed, half asleep, overworked and with very little interest in life (Liao 1948:98).

Seldom, if ever, was the apprentice systematically instructed, and almost never before the end of his first year. Thereafter he learned by observation and imitation, learning to do by doing.

He does things from his own observation exactly as done by his *shifu* [master]. Even the details must be followed to the letter. In most cases even the asking of a question is not allowed . . . even verbal transmissions are sometimes not present (Liao 1948:96).

Indeed, traditional Chinese master craftsmen reputedly deliberately concealed techniques from their apprentices, making sure that a newly graduated journeyman could not compete with them on equal terms. The newly graduated journeyman had a life's experience in which to learn the more subtle tricks of the trade on his own, but that experience only began after his apprenticeship ended. From the apprentice's point of view, his apprenticeship was a fee paid to gain entry into the trade and he really only began to learn after all the dues had been paid.

Even where the apprentice may have been 'lucky' enough to receive some instruction, his treatment was less than delicate:

Apprenticeship

When he [the apprentice] is seen making a mistake, no one sits down and talks it over with him. Immediately comes a kick or a slap in the face. After this, it is believed that the same mistake will not be repeated again. But if punishments of this kind are carried too far (which is often the case) and result in the escape, injury or even suicide on the part of the receiver, he is merely considered to be an unfortunate and unavoidable casualty in the struggle for existence . . . The death of a mere apprentice is not remembered for very long (Liao 1948: 101).

Despite its inefficiencies and brutality as regards instruction, apprenticeship nevertheless served for centuries as the institutionalized means of labor-force reproduction. Its rigors served to enforce the exclusive character of craft occupations in the traditional context, setting the skilled worker apart from the rabble and, despite substantial changes in craft production in recent history, its essential character remains quite similar.

Apprenticeship today remains a matter of contract between boss and guarantor. In fact, in order to secure an apprenticeship for myself as a base from which to pursue fieldwork, I was required to submit a letter from some respectable person setting out the terms under which I wished to work, and guaranteeing my adherence to those terms.* The contract seems to be somewhat less binding nowadays than it was in the earlier period. I witnessed two cases in which apprentices left the factory where I worked in the middle of their terms to complete their apprenticeships elsewhere. This was accepted by the boss with considerable disgust, but more or less as a matter over which he had no recourse.

The fact that the apprentice nowadays begins contributing to production almost immediately, earning his keep almost from the first day of his term, may have something to do with the fact that the boss can no longer demand that the guarantor reimburse him for room and board expenses when the apprentice fails to fulfill his contract terms. Perhaps the absence of a strong organization of proprietors in the industry capable of enforcing the terms of such contracts makes them less binding than in the heyday of highly organized guilds.

However, apprentice labor is not wasted nowadays on the kind of odious tasks unrelated to production described above by Liao. Apprentice labor is considered valuable if properly applied. While the tasks to which the apprentice is assigned are often monotonous because of the repetitious motions involved in executing large numbers of identical items such as table legs, these are never-

---

* In my case, the contract included the provision that I would work at the factory as a carver's apprentice for no wages, but with meals provided. While apprentices in present-day Hong Kong are usually paid a small wage of roughly H.K.$100–150 a month to start, the lack of wages in my case was a concession to the boss in exchange for the favor *he* was doing *me* by letting me work in his factory. A further concession involved my tutoring the boss's eldest son in English two afternoons a week as part of the package. The reluctance of Hong Kong craftsmen to teach their skills to a foreigner was a serious obstacle in my previous unsuccessful efforts to secure an apprenticeship.

theless productive tasks which are necessary to the functioning of the production unit, and which make it possible for the boss to avoid having to pay skilled workers high wages to accomplish simple operations. In addition, there is a sufficient variety of such tasks in the production of art-carved furniture requiring different assortments of techniques for the work to be far less monotonous than it must have been for Peking carpet apprentices of the 1920s, who performed a single operation for as many as fourteen hours a day for the entire duration of their terms (Ch'u and Blaisdell 1924:32).

Despite the demand for labor which has existed in the Hong Kong art-carved furniture industry since the early 1950s, training during the apprenticeship term has not become any more systematic or efficient than in the previous era. Once an apprentice has created a productive niche for himself, his fellow workers seldom bother to teach him anything further, particularly since the boss is usually loathe to see his skilled workers wasting time, for which he is paying them, on such marginally productive enterprises as teaching apprentices. In factories in which the boss pays wages by the piece, which were probably more prevalent in the early period of manufacture than at present, the pace of work is more a matter of the workers' whims, the boss being less concerned that he get every ounce of productivity out of each minute for which he is paying. A piecework factory may therefore be a more desirable setting, from the apprentice's point of view, in which to take up the craft (see Chapter 3 on piecework and day-wages).

Where the boss pays wages by the day, the apprentice may receive a few seconds of instruction when he brings a finished piece to his master who may or may not be the boss of the factory. With a few words of advice, the master pencils in areas that need correcting. Occasionally, in passing, one or another worker will stop at the apprentice's bench for a few seconds and comment on the apprentice's work or grab a tool and show the apprentice how it is done . . . again! or give some advice as to how to proceed, but these are usually stolen and precious moments, and more extensive discussion surely brings the boss around with a scolding for all concerned.

Workers are under close scrutiny of the boss to make sure they are producing at a good rate, particularly as they command a fairly decent wage in Hong Kong where labor is scarce. One worker was fired during the course of my apprenticeship for working too slowly. Carvers and carpenters, who might under other conditions be capable of turning out finer work and encouraging their apprentices to do so, are not usually good models for emulation. Nor for that matter are they very much in the mood to be emulated. The quality noted most frequently by today's workers as most important in their choice of apprentices was 'obedience' with 'willingness to learn' a distant second.

Apprentices in labor-scarce Hong Kong, however, command a bit more respect than they did in the earlier period, and Hong Kong laws which forbid the beating of apprentices are, according to the workers, occasionally enforced.

26

However, many workers seriously believe that the only way to get a boy to learn is to beat him as they had been beaten as apprentices. Indeed, several of my fellow workers expressed their regret to me that it was against the law to beat apprentices.

The prevalence of such ideas can make an apprentice's life pretty miserable even without beatings. There are many almost ritualized hard knocks that one must endure, and these are still often protracted if no longer brutal. In the course of time one learns to ignore abuse and appreciate neglect. The apprentice is still often scolded, lectured to on his shortcomings, ignored, given back work to finish properly with no instructions, deliberately prevented from watching his master correct whatever mistakes he may have made on work completed. At least one apprentice who entered the factory where I worked had left before I did. He had not enjoyed the experience.

However, for tougher young lads of fourteen—sixteen years of age, the daily routine, although rigorous, no longer entails many degrading chores unrelated to production, and is not completely devoid of opportunities for respite from repetitious semi-skilled work. During the lunch break there is usually a card game for small stakes to play or to watch, and at 3.15 p.m. another break occurs, during which coffee, tea or sodas, brought in from outside, are taken by the workers in the course of work, the pace of which abates for a while. Although most of his meagre pocket money is usually gambled away within one or two days after payday, the apprentice may occasionally treat himself to a soda, or on rare occasions may be the beneficiary of one or another worker's generosity.

On any given day there may be deliveries to make, and that means a ride out on a truck hired for the trip with the boss's son, or even alone, to deliver finished items to dealers in the tourist section. This normally takes the better part of the afternoon and, while often entailing hard work moving heavy furniture, breaks the monotony of continuous factory work. It may also give the apprentice some time for private recreation while he makes his way back to his palet in the factory by public transportation.

Since the introduction of power-driven machines did not directly affect the skills of carving, the carving slots in the division of labor which characterized manufacture remained intact as carpentry became mechanized. A carver's apprenticeship today, therefore, remains rather similar to what it must have been like in the early days of manufacture. While manufacture was characterized by an elaborated division of labor in carving, with separate niches for carvers of superior artistic skill (rough-carvers) and simple technicians (smooth-carvers), no class of totally unskilled laborers was created, as often occurred elsewhere in association with manufacture. The grades of skill in the carving labor force represented by the separate niches for two types of carvers, however, still make it possible for a newly graduated journeyman carver to participate effectively in the division of labor with a narrower range of skill. A carver's apprentice begins his learning experiences in smooth-carving, and must be very lucky to learn any rough-carving by the time his three-year term is up.

For the carver's apprentice, among the most important events of his apprenticeship is the acquisition, by gradual accretion, of his own set of carving tools and, perhaps more important, acquisition of the skills of caring for them. Meticulous care of one's tools is the hallmark of the accomplished craftsman, and only when one has learned these skills is it possible even to conceive of working independently of one's master.

From the first day of his apprenticeship, the carver's apprentice is fitted out with a minimum tool kit from the kit of his master. A carver may have twenty—thirty tools in service at any one time, with perhaps another twenty in reserve. It is from this reserve stock of his master that the apprentice is first supplied, the master expecting that the tools will be returned when the apprentice eventually acquires some of his own.

One opportunity which an apprentice has to do this is during the occasional visits of an itinerant carving-tool salesman, who makes the rounds from carving factory to carving factory on a seemingly irregular schedule. When he arrives, all hands gather round, sorting through his wares which he displays on the floor laid out on a cloth pad. Workers will select a few tools, and an apprentice, if he still has any of his small wage left, can purchase a few. If, as is more likely, the apprentice is penniless, he may take an advance from the boss towards the purchase of his own tool kit, either from the itinerant salesman, or at one of several locations throughout Hong Kong where they are made. In 1972—3, tools ranged in price from just over H.K$3 to H.K$8.

There are many different tools, varied in shape and size of blade, for use in carving wood at different angles and with different effect. There are flat chisels of several sizes, chisels with varying degrees of curvature, L-shaped chisels, and V-shaped groovers (see Figure 1).

Because of the many different shapes of tools, a carver requires an assortment of sharpening stones, which are also his own personal property. This is particularly important for curved-edge tools. A carver will always have at least one stone in which there are many well-worn grooves that fit exactly the curvature of his own tools. Thus when an apprentice begins to acquire his own curved-edge tools he must also acquire his own stones in which to begin the particularly distinctive grooves to match his tools.

In my experience, it was the V-shaped groover that was the last addition to the apprentice's kit. Learning to keep a proper edge on it takes an enormous amount of patience and skill. It took me the better part of a year just to begin to get the hang of it. Good groovers are essential in every smooth-carver's outfit and are very hard to come by. Only made in one or two places in Hong Kong, many are substandard and break and chip frequently in the course of work. They must be sharpened many times over, a particularly painstaking operation, which is often a source of some annoyance to the workers. Groovers are the

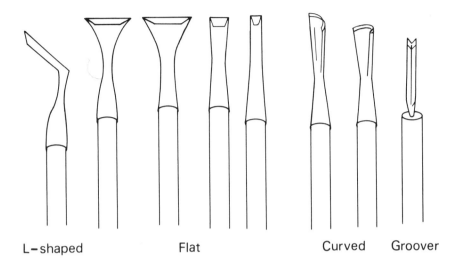

L-shaped   Flat   Curved   Groover

Figure 1. Types of carving tools

most costly of the tools in a carver's kit, but many workers will give up trying
to keep a substandard tool in shape, and cast about among acquaintances or at
various shops to buy another.

Much of the work to which an apprentice is first assigned requires the use of
a good groover. Until he acquires his own, the apprentice must use one of his
master's groovers, and will rely on his master to keep it fit for use.

At first, with some supervision and rude coachings from his master, the
apprentice begins the task of learning to shape handles for his tools, to sharpen
their blades and to care for them properly. After an initial cast off, he is left
mostly on his own, except when he makes a serious mistake which might result
in the destruction of someone else's property, such as his master's tools or
sharpening stones. At times like these, he is severely scolded, reinstructed,
supervised for a short period, and is then back on his own again. Within six
months to a year he can properly care for all the tools in his kit without supervision, and is ready to begin to acquire some of his own.

For the carver's apprentice there is an initial period of great and rather
continuous pain associated with his early learning efforts, because his hands have
not yet swelled and hardened to the punishment inflicted on them by the
wooden handles of the carving tools. The apprentice pushes his tools trying to
be oblivious of the pain, and after several weeks his hands have hardened suf-
ficiently so that physical hardship is no longer a factor in his learning. From

that point on, for the next two years, there is a great deal of repetitious semi-skilled drudgery to keep the apprentice occupied.

For days on end as an apprentice, I would see nothing cross my bench but table legs, literally by the hundreds. They were rough-carved out and passed on to me the smooth-carve. After turning out fifty or so, one feels competent to deal with them, but they keep coming with no end in sight. By the time I left the factory I could do sixty-four in a nine-hour day, having thus created a niche for a semi-skilled laborer in the division of labor.

Only on very rare occasions, when there is quite literally nothing else to occupy him, will an apprentice be given a chance to try his hand in finishing a particularly elaborately rough-carved item. Only a very indulgent master will go so far as to teach his apprentice to rough-carve, this being more likely to occur if the apprentice is learning the trade from his father.

Of forty-seven apprentices questioned in the course of my survey, twenty-three had followed their fathers into the trade. Second, third and fourth generation carving families occur with greatest frequency among Zhejiang workers and bosses, whose livelihood was at one time tied to the pre-revolutionary trade centered around Shanghai. Newcomers to Hong Kong in the early 1950s, they tended to take apprentices from within a closer circle of relations than the more numerous Cantonese workers of the period. Of the forty-seven apprentices mentioned above, thirteen were of Zhejiang extraction, and nine of these thirteen were learning the trade from their fathers. Of the remaining thirty-four Cantonese apprentices, only fourteen had followed their fathers into the trade.

Upon graduation, most carvers, although they own a portion of the means of production, are incapable of operating independently of the production unit in which they have been trained, or independently of other similar units of the Hong Kong art-carved furniture industry. They have been trained only so as to be able to occupy the less highly skilled smooth-carver's niche in the more elaborate 'manufacturing' division of labor.

Within the furniture industry as it has expanded, diversified and become more highly capitalized, it has been in carpentry that the greater proportion of capital and labor power has been concentrated. While the newly graduated carver's apprentice still owns his own tools, the furniture industry into which he graduates is finding less and less use for his skills. The carpenter, who no longer owns his own tools, is nevertheless in greater demand in the now more diversified furniture industry, and has the added advantage of being able to sell his skills outside the furniture industry in Hong Kong society at large. This circumstance contributes to the prevailing opinion among carvers that their job is a dead-end occupation, and makes carpentry more attractive to a wider range of young boys seeking a vocation with a secure future.

While carpentry has not yet become simply a matter of machining pieces of wood into the right shapes and sizes and slapping them together, and while apprentices must still acquire a certain degree of skill in the use of traditional hand-tools, more and more specialized machine-tools are coming to undermine and replace those skills, as carpentry becomes progressively more automated and its division of labor progressively more elaborated.

This has made it possible for the boss effectively to employ more specialized, less highly skilled laborers in production, and indeed one could argue that the uniform motion of the power-driven machine blade, by replacing the hand of the skilled artisan, has begun to turn carpentry into child's play. The increasing use of semi-skilled apprentice labor in the carpentry area of production gives weight to such an argument. My survey crew encountered nearly twice as many carpenter's apprentices as carver's apprentices in the course of administering questionnaires to workers in the industry.

As a greater proportion of capital is now sunk into carpentry, and as it is now easier for semi-skilled apprentice labor power to fill niches in the carpentry area, bosses have naturally expanded their recruitment endeavors in carpentry. This is manifest in figures that show that only ten out of thirty carpenters' apprentices questioned had followed their fathers into the carpentry trade, while a much higher proportion, eleven out of sixteen carvers' apprentices interviewed, had followed their fathers into carving. It might be concluded from these figures that carpentry apprentices are now recruited from among a wider circle of workers' relations. In carving, where the market for carvers' skills has remained constant, or declined relative to the total labor market in the furniture industry, familial particularism has risen in importance in retaining the relatively fewer available positions for skilled carvers within a narrower circle of workers' relations.

Within the same art-carved furniture industry, therefore, particularism as a factor in recruiting apprentices exists with differing levels of intensity at different positions in the division of labor, varying according to the ways in which the introduction of new technology manifested itself with respect to those different positions, and with the differing effects and consequences of that introduction on the demand for different kinds of labor power.

In the early 1950s, when the manufacturing division of labor was consolidated, skills in carving were graded, as two kinds of carvers made their appearance in a division of labor which included more generalized carpenters. The introduction of machines led to the downgrading of required skills, but this time in carpentry. The further downgrading which has recently occurred in carving is a product of the growing insignificance of the carved portions of furniture in a now more diverse market, rather than of any direct impact of machines on the skills required of carving.

Thus, although arising as the result of different factors in each instance, elaboration of the division of labor in both carving and carpentry has created more specialized niches for more narrowly skilled workmen, undermining the skills of traditional hand craftsmen by making it possible for less highly skilled workers to contribute effectively to production. As a consequence, less time and effort need be expended in the training of apprentices, and a portion of the traditional apprenticeship period has become superfluous. The necessary costs of reproducing labor power in the industry have thereby been decreased. This implies a fall in the value of the workers' labor power and an increase in surplus value accruing to capital since 'everything that shortens the necessary labor time required for the reproduction of labor power extends the domain of surplus labor' (Marx 1967:1:350).

The diminution of the necessary labor time and expansion of the domain of surplus labor may find institutional expression in different ways. Where areas of worker expertise become extremely narrow and specialized, that is, where the level of skill and necessary labor time required to reproduce it diminish to the vanishing point, the persistence of a long apprenticeship, rather than protecting the value of workers' labor power, may come to serve as an institutionalized means of naked exploitation, by providing unpaid labor on contract for the entire period of the apprentice's term. Ch'u and Blaisdell (1924:34) describe a situation prevailing in the carpet industry of Peking in the 1920s where 78 workshops employed 1,373 apprentices and not a single 'workman'. Increasing use of apprentice labor in the carpentry section of art-carved furniture factories is a similar phenomenon, although not likely to be carried to such extremes. The level of skill required of carpenters in the art-carved furniture industry has not degenerated to an extent which would make it possible for apprentices, if not working in a context which included at least a majority of skilled artisans, to turn out the product adequately.

Such exploitative arrangements may also be forestalled by traditional guild rules strictly limiting the number of apprentices a master may employ at one time, or by the intervention of organized labor which may prevent such unbridled exploitation of apprentice labor. Under such conditions the potential for extension of the domain of surplus labor may not be so great, and the struggle between capital and labor for control over the quality and quantity of labor power reproduced is manifest in a different institutional context, although the interests of workers in preserving the value of their labor power continue to be served by restricting the number of apprentices, and therefore the rate at which apprentices are graduated.

Among a new generation of bosses in the art-carved furniture industry, the idea has already taken hold that the term of apprenticeship needs to be streamlined and shortened in duration. A shorter apprenticeship term would result in a readjustment in the supply of workers favorable to capital. If allowed to create labor force members at a higher rate of apprentice turnover, the bosses would increase their supply of laborers, and labor costs would drop correspondingly or remain constant as the industry expanded.

It is clearly in the interests of workers under such conditions to reduce the rate of apprentice turnover and to insist upon a long period of apprenticeship as a means of protecting the value of their labor power (Marx 1967:1:367).

32

Apprenticeship

It is not surprising that organized labor in the art-carved furniture industry has thus far resisted any tampering with the length of the apprenticeship term. What is perhaps a little unusual is how well disposed the Woodwork Carvers' Union is to fight to maintain the preponderant influence of skilled labor in the industry against the tendency for mechanization and specialization to cheapen its members' labor power (see Chapter 5).

Precisely because of its pro-communist stance, however, the union also stands committed to ridding society of the remnants of its 'feudal' past. It is therefore not inconceivable that the union could accept a streamlining and shortening of the apprenticeship term. However, it would seem to require on their part the proviso that training be systematic, and involve the carpenters' apprentices particularly in learning all aspects of the construction of furniture.

While the deterioration of the carver's position in the industry is determined by market forces beyond the union's control, it would seem that the all-round skill of its carpenter members could be preserved within a regime of *systematic* apprenticeship training over a period of two years, or perhaps less.

For their part, young apprentices are always eager to graduate early, and a shortened term would encourage more boys to take up apprenticeships in the industry. In the long run, however, the faster the bosses can turn out apprentices, the lower will the value of labor power become in the industry, and the lower the wage that newly graduated journeymen can command.

How the union will choose to deal with this question will undoubtedly be decided in the next few years, when the bosses begin to change the length and content of the apprenticeship term. It is, in any event, unlikely that factory and shop owners will be able to take advantage of all the potentialities for expanding the domain of surplus labor made possible by the decrease in necessary labor time required for the reproduction of their labor power. Their ability to make full use in production of the increasingly narrow specialization which technology allows will undoubtedly be limited by the well-defended interests of workers which lie in protecting the value of their still rather highly skilled labor power.

Insofar as apprenticeship plays a key role in determining the quantity, quality, and hence value of that labor power, it occupies a strategic position as an object of struggle between labor and capital in the transition from craft to industry.

3

Organization and relations of production

In order to discuss the organization and relations of production of the art-carved furniture industry, one further observation must be made concerning the properties of 'manufacture'.

Since the different operations of which the manufacturing division of labor consists require unequal periods of time for their performance, and therefore in equal times yield unequal quantities of fractional products, 'there must be a different number of laborers for each operation'. The division of labor characteristic of manufacture therefore 'not only simplifies and multiplies the qualitatively different parts' of the labor process, 'but also creates a fixed mathematical relation or ratio which regulates the quantitative extent of those parts — i.e. the relative number of laborers, or the relative size of the group of laborers for each detail operation' (Marx 1967:346—6).

Thus it was noted in Chapter 1 that production units in the art-carved furniture industry in the 1950s maintained roughly the same proportions of practitioners in each stage of the production process, carving, carpentry and painting, and that factory owners with greater capital assets hired larger numbers of workers in roughly the same proportions. While the mathematical relation or ratio between carvers, carpenters and painters would presumably differ for different products of the furniture industry, I think it fair to assume, as I have found no evidence of factory specialization in particular products, that product mix represented in the orders of most factories is fairly uniform. There is therefore good cause to assume that the proportions of craft practitioners in each stage of the production process has also been fairly uniform from production unit to production unit within the art-carved furniture industry.

The present chapter is concerned to establish the specific requirements of art-carved furniture and camphorwood chests production as regards capital and labor in its various niches necessary for competitive operation. It should be noted that it is possible in the Hong Kong based art-carved furniture industry to operate a production unit below the capital and labor threshold necessary for competitive operation. Firms of lesser size continue to function by locking into the division of labor of larger competitive firms, and may operate at a

34

smaller margin of profit. While the prices which these smaller firms are paid for delivered merchandise is determined by the average productivity of the industry as a whole, which they are not often able to match, independent 'firms' with as few as a single worker participate in various segments of the production process of larger production units, and may thereby secure the livelihood of a family.

As my data for the capital and labor requirements for competitive operation are more detailed for the period 1972–3, I have chosen to discuss those requirements first. I shall also refer to known events in the history of the industry to establish such requirements for the period of manufacture.

Heng Lung Co. may be taken as exemplary of the relative proportions of craft practitioners in a minimum unit of competitive operation. There, the proportions were roughly 4 rough-carvers: 4 smooth-carvers: 3 carpenters: 1 painter. During my stay, Heng Lung Co. never employed a full-time painter, although a painter was occasionally hired by the day for special-order items which were crated and exported direct from the factory, independent of any retailer. However, as much of the painting, varnishing and finishing of the merchandise produced in the industry is done in retail outlets in accord with customers' tastes, painting may be more usefully considered as an adjunct of marketing rather than of production *per se*. In this sense, it is not absolutely necessary to maintain a painter full time in one's production unit to operate competitively. However, I believe the quantity of merchandise produced by Heng Lung Co., which was normally shipped out to retail outlets in the raw, was sufficient to have merited the services of at least a single full-time painter/varnisher. In any case, the proportion of carvers to carpenters is the crucial one in the production end of the business.

Carvers

The proportion of rough- to smooth-carvers in a modern factory, 4:4 or 1:1, has been roughly the same for quite some time. It is probably an artifact of craft 'manufacture', a response to increased demand for output from abroad, within the limits of a hand-powered technology. It is conceivable, but unproved, that the rough–smooth division of carvers goes back even further in time. While there is no direct evidence of this in the production of wood-carvings prior to the stimulus of western demand for carved furniture, Herman found that many traditional Chinese craftsmen, although using hand-powered tools, were also often part of an assembly line process of production (Herman 1954:1). Such a formulation is consistent with a 'high level equilibrium trap' model of the economy of late Ch'ing dynasty China (see Elvin 1973:314), in which the Chinese economy is described as using most of its contemporary energy sources to the limits of contemporary technological efficiency, which was considerable, and fairly well entrenched. A sure sign of this condition in crafts of that day would have been the elaboration of the division of labor in craft production like that described by Herman. It is altogether conceivable that rural temple carvers operated within a rough–smooth division of labor before being hired into coastal furniture factories.

Stanley maintains that the traditional Chinese carver did not use the V-shaped groover which is the smooth-carvers' most-used implement today. This may indicate that smooth-carving did not exist as a separate niche prior to the opportunities afforded by overseas markets (Stanley 1914:82). But it seemed inconceivable to me in the context of contemporary carving that the traditional Chinese carver did not employ a V-shaped tool. There are some wonderfully delicate motifs that I think cannot be executed without it. I cite Stanley's own plates as evidence of work with a V-tool (e.g. Stanley:1914, facing p. 82). However, it is possible that its use goes back only 200 years or so to the earlier, more bureaucratically controlled, export furniture trade centering around the port of trade of Canton in the late seventeenth and early eighteenth centuries.

In any case, by 1950 in Hong Kong, a 1:1 ratio of rough- to smooth-carvers (who did use a V-tool) served as the norm for the manufacture of carved-wood products. This ratio survived the technological inputs of the early 1960s, and is still maintained. It is not unusual today to find a rough- and a smooth-carver working as a team, the rough-carver usually, although not always, senior in age. If one member of the team decides to move to another factory to work, he will normally try to make arrangements for his partner to move as well. The relation between such partners is always one of profound friendship. It is said that in early post-war Hong Kong, the wages earned from the produce of one such team were divided 60:40, 60% to the rough-carver and 40% to the smooth-carver, but in my experience, the boss enters into a separate wage agreement with each individual worker. A fine smooth-carver may make as much as a mediocre rough-carver, although the former would not usually be found working with the latter as a team.

The carver's tool kit has not changed at all in the past 25 years, and probably not very much in the 200 years before that. What Hommel (1937:250, Fig. 370) calls 'carpenter's forming tools' are easily recognizable as present-day rough-carver's chisels (see Plate 4), with a characteristically short handle, flattened by the constant application of a hammer. Smooth-carver's chisel handles are usually longer and more gracile as they are applied only with hand, or sometimes shoulder, power. Well-worn, smooth-carving tool handles are often quite beautiful, as they are always fashioned by the carver himself from scraps of high-grade furniture wood, which become highly polished from the constant application of the carver's hands.

The difference in form between rough- and smooth-carver's tool handles presents a very concrete example of how the division of labor characteristic of manufacture begets 'a differentiation of the instruments of labor — a differentiation whereby implements of a given sort acquire fixed shapes, adapted to each particular application'. The elaboration of the division of labor 'simplifies,

4. Rough-carver's tools

improves and multiplies the implements of labor by adapting them to the exclusively special functions of each detail laborer' (Marx 1967:341 quoted in Dobb 1947:145). Here, changes in the division of labor (relations of production) directly affect the shape of the means (the forces) of production.

This simplification, improvement and multiplication of the implements of labor characteristically provided 'one of the material conditions for the existence of machinery, which consists of a combination of simple instruments' (Marx 1967:342).

In the art-carved furniture industry, the elaboration of the division of labor which occurred in carving, however, proved to be a dead end. Rather than fastening on the already elaborated division of labor in carving, technological change was instituted in the art-carved furniture industry in the more generalized carpentry niches, leaving the carving slots in the division of labor unaffected by power-driven blades. It is probable that unlike ivory-carving, wood-carving in relief just does not lend itself well to work with a rapidly rotating dentist-drill-like tool blade, which has become standard equipment in the production of ivory carvings.

Power-driven machinery has begun to be used in the preparation of certain abstract motifs in rosewood, which is not usually so elaborately or deeply carved as teak and camphorwood, but the machines do not replace the rough- and

37

smooth-carvers. They simply aid in removing excess wood to a uniform depth before carving commences. This is helpful in carving the harder rosewoods, and the machines are a recent development there, but they are not viable in the complex relief-carving of human and animal figures so elaborately represented in the more easily carved teakwood.

However, these 'carving machines' do show that the development of new technological devices is an empirical and creative process which is ongoing. The first such machines were apparently devised by workers in the rosewood industry and designed to their own specifications. At present, the creative process is not likely to go much further in teakwood and camphorwood carving, quite apart from the technical problems involved, since many of the carved-furniture producing firms have diversified into modern furniture and are placing less emphasis on carving in their marketing. The carving niches of the division of labor remain unchanged, although the wave of technological inputs into carpentry has reduced the significance of the carvers to the industry as a whole.

A few other tools in the carver's kit need to be mentioned. The hammer employed in rough-carving is really a kind of small mallet. It is short handled, with a steel, sometimes bronze head that looks very much like an unsharpened tomahawk blank. A rough-carver's hand takes up most of the short wood handle and the steel head is grasped rather like a table tennis bat (see Figure 2). The hatchet is used to hit, or, more properly, tap, the back of the carving tool, forcing the blade into the wood. The tool is tapped, withdrawn, set, tapped again, withdrawn, reset, tapped again with great rapidity, with the wrist and forearm providing most of the motion of the mallet. Several rough-carvers working together make quite a din, tap-tapping in counterpoint.

Another tool which has been part of the carver's kit, at least since Ming times (1368–1644), is the wire saw, which is today more frequently encountered in working rosewood, but which is sometimes required in occasional teakwood pieces. It is employed in a manner similar to the western coping saw for cutting out lattice work designs in wood. Stanley describes the traditional preparation of this formidable tool:

The wire saw for fretwork used by the Chinese seems a more businesslike tool than the European, the wire being kept tense between the ends of a bent semi-circle of a substantial segment of bamboo. The carver prepares his own wire by means of a more highly tempered steel chisel; this saw enables the worker to get through his work at great speed and gives him easy control when changing the direction of the cut (Stanley 1914:82).

The wire saw is prepared in precisely the same manner nowadays. It is primarily carvers of long experience who are capable enough to manage the delicate preparation. On occasion, when my own master was called upon to execute motifs which required use of a wire saw, his fellow workers would tauntingly spread out perhaps an extra three to four feet as he prepared to

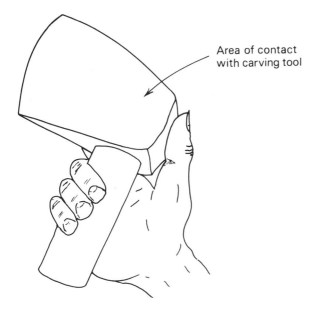

Area of contact
with carving tool

Figure 2. Carver's mallet in hand

nick the taut wire. A poorly executed nick could have caused the wire to pop and the bamboo to whip the wire about in a dangerous fashion. My master's fellow workers took no chances and made a show of it.

All these tools in a carver's kit are his own personal property. The only equipment supplied by a factory owner to a carver working in his employ, in addition to raw materials, is a work bench (see Plate 1).

Work is performed by both rough-carver and smooth-carver on the near half of the bench which is solid wood; the recessed portion holds the carver's tools and is often covered entirely by a piece of work in execution, the carver setting all the carving tools he may require on the face of the piece being prepared.

The rough-carver begins work on a blank piece of wood, which has been cut to size and prepared in the carpentry section of the shop using a variety of power saws and planing machines. The pieces vary in size from 12 in. x 16 in. x ½ in. for the less elaborately carved back and side panels of camphorwood chests to 3 ft x 2 ft x 2 in. boards destined to become sumptuously carved coffee table tops (see Plate 3).

Some rough-carvers will sketch their work out in pencil or marking-pen prior to commencing carving. Others will simply plan out the design in their minds and begin carving without so much as a mark on the wood. One would imagine that the latter might be the most highly skilled, most experienced craftsmen. However, at least one of the most highly skilled carvers I was to meet during my fieldwork (see Chapter 8), most of whose work consisted of special-order pieces, was quite meticulous in his pencil sketches. It is probable that most rough-carvers are capable of turning out a number of standard repertoire items without prior sketching, but require aids in the execution of more demanding projects.

The rough-carver removes large chunks of wood around what will become the principal figures and characters of the carving, creating a relief effect in which the characters stand out. He also removes wood in more delicate fashion from the principal characters themselves, establishing their proportions, their costume and their bearing. He blocks out the setting as well, background and foreground, trees, pavilions, battlegrounds, pagodas, bridges, etc., before passing the piece to the smooth-carver (Plate 1 shows a rough-carver in action).

In the hands of the smooth-carver, the carving assumes its final shape. Excess wood is removed without the aid of the mallet, the lines are sharpened up, the background and foreground receiving their final detail and line work with a V-shaped groover, and the faces and the costumes of the characters given their final flourish (Plate 2 shows a smooth-carver in action).

The relationship between boss and carver is not very different from that which existed when art-carved furniture was first 'manufactured' in urban Shanghai. The boss contracts with the carver for the use of the carver's skilled labor power. The carver retains ownership of a portion of the mechanism of production (his tool kit), and is almost in that sense on equal terms with the boss. He is selling his labor power, but is also selling the use of required capital goods, namely his tools of the trade. He is still an independent artisan, although now dependent to a larger extent on the continued prosperity of the carved-furniture industry.

The carver's behavior in production is marked by a lack of industrial discipline which is often encountered in the work habits of former peasants working in industry (Shih 1944:64). Such work behavior may also be taken to typify that of the intractable skilled worker in a period of manufacture before the intro-duction of the uniform motion of machine blades and the discipline that such uniform motion demands. In manufacture, the workers with their own tools constitute in and of themselves the mechanism of manufacture. Thus, 'through-out the whole manufacturing period there runs the complaint of want of discipline among the workmen' (Marx 1967:367). P. T. Lau attests to the presence of such a work pattern in the jade industry of Canton:

One who visits the workshops cannot help but be impressed by the number of vacancies or absent workmen. They go out for a walk, or to take tea perhaps once in every hour. They calculate to earn only a certain sum per day and when that minimum is reached, they work no more (Lau 1918:356).

Today such tendencies are still prevalent among highly skilled carvers. Workers, especially bachelors, will take afternoons off to have tea, to visit friends at other factories or to play mah-jong. Family men with more responsibilities tend to work more steadily, some for as many as 7 nine-hour days a week. Most workers can do well enough working 5½ to 6 such days a week, particularly if other members of their households are wage-earners. Additional household income might be expected to result in increased leisure for the carver head of houshold, meaning more tea breaks, more mah-jong afternoons, etc.

Special expenses, such as those associated with marriage or accumulated gambling debts, may require a conscientious household head or single worker to exert himself to his limits, 7 days a week, but labor scarcity until very recently has meant relatively high wages for carvers, and most take advantage of the high cost of their labor power by not working too much. They are still the refractory class of the manufacturing period of the 1950s, although they are now more dependent on production units of greatly expanded capital. A carver needs more than just his carving tools to run an establishment competitively today.* The still characteristic dream of the artisan to be his own boss (see Engels 1959: 464) is now more than ever beyond fulfilment.

Carpentry

The reader has already had a glimpse of how expanding capital requirements influenced carpentry with respect to skills of the trade and recruitment (see Chapter 2). The introduction of machines into carpentry, however, also changed the established ratio of carvers to carpenters.

Whereas today a ratio of 8 carvers: 3 carpenters: 1 painter has been posited as the minimum for a competitive production unit, prior to the technological inputs of the 1960s, this ratio was probably more like 8:6:1, and more probably 16:12:2 for competitive operation at that time.

It is clear from the following figures that larger capital requirements in the 1960s made possible a reduction in the total number of workers required per production unit for those bosses who could afford the installation of expensive capital machines.

According to Table 1, in 1953 there were close to fifty workers per unit, which supports the suggestion above that the minimum number of workers for competitive operation at that time was about thirty. By 1963, or shortly after the introduction of power-tools, figures tend to show a smaller worker:unit ratio as being most common. This proportion decreased steadily to the present day. The table shows that the labor requirements of a production unit diminished from somewhere around thirty workers to about ten workers after ten years of continued application of machine power to production.

At present, in the larger production units, there are all kinds of innovative possibilities for the use of more, and more varied, modern machines in a more elaborate division of labor, producing more modern-style, less elaborately carved

* For exception, see Chapter 8.

The wood-carvers of Hong Kong

Table 1. *Number of workers employed per production unit (incidence) 1953–73*

	1–5	6–10	11–20	21–50	51–100	100+
1953	1	0	1	1	3	0
1963	2	1	8	9	0	0
1968	3	5	11	9	0	1
1973	18	18	15	8	2	2

furniture. The proliferation of such units with significantly greater capital and labor requirements could very well lead to the introduction of full-scale mass production of contemporary furniture, and significantly alter the minimum requirements of competitive operation in the furniture industry. It is these larger units which will be the competitive units of furniture production in the future, but they have only just taken hold.

In 1972–3 a competitive unit could still get by with three carpenters, who employed the following minimum of power-driven tools: one table saw, one band saw, one planing machine, one sanding machine, one drill press, one electric spot welder for repairing band-saw blades and other hand tools, and one electric grinding wheel for sharpening tool blades.

All these machines require a capital investment of several hundreds of thousands of Hong Kong dollars and tend to divide capital and labor to a larger degree than ever before. While carvers still own a portion of the means of production, the significance of that portion relative to total capital outlay has declined enormously. The carpenter has been all but stripped of the required tools of his trade. He is now more than ever a proletarian in permanent wage servitude to the furniture-producing capitalist. However, work relations seem to mitigate to a certain extent this growing separation between worker and employer.

While the carpenter no longer has anything to sell but his labor at the boss's machines, it is still very likely that his boss will also be a fellow worker, or former fellow worker, either carver or carpenter. Today, in spite of expanding capital requirements, there is still a senior generation of factory bosses, such as my own boss at Heng Lung Co., who at one time were workers themselves and who continue to work alongside their workers. Roughly 75% of all workers questioned (n = 226) said that their bosses worked along with them in the factory. 83% of factory bosses questioned (n = 36) said that they continued to work as laborers along with their workers.

Such work arrangements have been held to have had a profound effect on social relations within the production unit in the traditional Chinese economic setting. Gamble states:

Wages are the principal thing in which the workers are interested, and they are usually adjusted by the employers without any special demand from their employees. *The relationship between the employers and employees is so close* that the employers are able to recognize when their employees need a higher wage to meet higher prices, and they are usually willing to grant it of their own accord. Seldom, if ever, is there an attempt on the part of workers to raise wages unless the price of living has gone up. They have a regular standard of living and do not often attempt to improve that standard, but they do fight against any attempt to reduce it (Gamble 1921:170, emphasis added).

Nowadays, the gap between bosses and workers has widened considerably. However, workers whom I came to know pretty well in the Woodwork Carvers' Union still expressed a preference for working for an employer who is also a worker, and who therefore better understands the needs of his workers. It is conceivable that boss—worker relations under such work conditions may maintain some of the traditional looseness which Gamble describes. It is also conceivable that the laboring boss is today freer with the fringe benefits to which workers often came to feel entitled in pre-manufacturing times, and which have been grouped under the heading of protectionist privileges in Chapter 1. There it was stated that the cost of workers' loyalty to a firm in a labor-scarce situation was high, and that bosses attempted to secure their labor supply by making certain concessions to their workers.

A strike which occurred in 1951 at George Zee Co. was no doubt attributable to the threatened removal of certain of the workers' prerogatives by Labor Department inspectors — namely the privileges of sleeping and gambling on the factory premises (see Commissioner of Labor, 1951—2:33—5; see also Chapter 5). The strike shows clearly that the workers were very touchy about any tampering with their customary privileges and may explain why, today, one still finds workers sleeping and gambling on factory premises. 70% of factory bosses questioned (n = 37) said that one or more of his workers slept in his factory. A significant portion of these bosses denied this was a factor in calculating workers' wages. Food is not so often provided nowadays, although there are numerous demands of other kinds on the boss's largesse, the fulfilling of which still helps a boss to maintain a traditional closeness to his labor force and keeps his workers content.

There is no question that the *de facto* privilege of workers to gamble on factory premises is still in effect. Gambling is endemic in the carved-furniture industry. There is nothing peculiar to the production of carved-wood furniture that should make this so. Nor do I believe that gambling occurs to any greater or lesser degree at any given organizational or technological moment in industrial development or in association with any given mode of production (see Huizinga 1950:3). However, gambling occupied so great a part of the leisure of so many workers in so many forms, both in and out of the factory, that it merits treatment in detail. It will also serve to introduce the most significant area of protectionist privilege in this industry today, the provision by bosses to workers of interest-free loans.

43

The wood-carvers of Hong Kong

If there is a national sport in Hong Kong, mah-jong is certainly it. Even apprentices dissipate their meager earnings at the mah-jong parlors in the first one or two days after payday. This is not restricted to apprentices, since virtually all workers have played mah-jong at one time or another, it being merely a question of how often in each case. At Heng Lung Co., mah-jong was not played as often as at some other factories known to me. Only on occasion would workers take an afternoon off to play with their fellow workers. I cannot vouch for how often each worker played upon arriving home after a normal day's work, but if furniture workers are similar to other Hong Kong residents it must have been often. The constant clatter of mah-jong tiles is part of the background noise on most Hong Kong streets. Mah-jong is, however, not the only outlet for the worker to dissipate his hard-earned wages according to the dictates of chance.

One old carver acquaintance of mine of consummate skill with the carving tool, with whom I worked at Heng Lung Co. and who later moved to Macau to take up wood-carving there, would budget $300 of the $900–1,000 a month he earned to gamble – horses, dogs, the Macau lottery, mah-jong, various card games, etc. Most workers were not so meticulous in their budgeting, and workers with families to support usually gambled with less abandon than my old carver friend, but his example does give some idea of the central place of gambling in workers' lives, and they have more or less established the use of the factory premises for such practices as a right. In the past, this may have been more of a privilege bestowed by the boss, but once established such privileges are difficult to rescind.

In the spring and fall the racing seasons open, horse racing in Hong Kong, and dog racing in Macau. Bets are openly solicited in the factory and phoned in on the factory phone when the boss is out, or when he himself may have some money riding on a big race. On Saturdays the radio in the factory blares out the races all day long and the workers listen attentively as their nags win or lose. A big handicap race invariably arouses great interest and great wagers. Fascination with the races is so great that very often workers spend a weekend, or, as in the case of my old carver friend, an entire working life in Macau to bet on the races, and to take advantage of the many other legal gambling outlets that Macau offers. Much money was won and lost by workers at Heng Lung Co. in the casinos.

Apart from the big money games, there is gambling for lower stakes which occurs on the factory floor during the lunch hour, or during breaks in piece-work routine. Almost invariably some game of cards is played from 12.50 to 1.30 or 1.40 after workers have finished their lunch and before they go back to work. While no money changes hands across the table, in deference to legal ordinances, debts are settled afterwards according to a record kept by one of the players.

At Heng Lung Co. two games were played – *sap m wu* (fifteen lakes) and *sap saam cheung* (thirteen cards). Fifteen lakes is a game resembling dominoes and proceeds with a great hullabulloo around the table. Each time a card is played, it is announced by its player together with the appropriate card with which the next player must follow. By the end of the round, the level of noise can get very high and the rhythm of play extremely animated. There is almost always a small crowd hanging around, among whom a long-winded discussion usually occurs at the end of a round as to how the cards might have been better played.

Thirteen cards is a game in which one must make the best arrangement of thirteen cards in ascending order of value in groups of 3–5–5 cards each. It is played with a standard western card deck, unlike fifteen lakes, by no more than four players at a time, usually for stakes much higher than the 10¢ H.K. per point of fifteen lakes. A great deal of money may change hands in thirteen cards, which in many other respects resembles poker. This game was played less often in Heng Lung Co. than fifteen lakes, and less often than in other factories.

It is of no significance to the boss, apart from the demands of Labor Department inspectors (and perhaps police), if the workers gamble on his premises on their own time. What is of significance to him is that it is *he* who often becomes the central source of worker credit. Most workers will clear their gambling debts with advances on their salaries from the boss and work off their debt by installments. In many cases, the boss ends up financing the workers' hard luck. However, the boss's generosity is not only relied upon to clear gambling debts, but is also mobilized to meet urgent needs of a family and ceremonial nature. Loans on the occasion of the marriage of a worker, for example, are still listed by workers as a use to which advances from the boss are put, and such occasions may have been a time of borrowing from one's boss in traditional times as well.

Both workers and bosses agree that workers may fall into debt to a boss of upwards of H.K.$3,000 – three or four months' wages in 1972–3. Several factory bosses very frankly discussed loans to workers as being instrumental in holding workers to their factories, in keeping them working, in securing required labor power by helping workers to clear debts at other factories, as well as mentioning the family and ceremonial needs of workers. Also significant in their accounts was the lending of money to workers to finance trips back to China to visit relatives in their native villages. My master at Heng Lung Co. made the trip several times a year to visit his wife and children, and was at times in debt to the boss for as much as H.K.$2,500.

About half of the workers who admitted to being in debt to their bosses were in debt for minor sums of from H.K.$100–300. This may be taken to represent the first level of boss's tolerance, which the largest number of workers are willing to exploit according to their immediate needs, gambling or otherwise. Beyond one month's wage, or about H.K.$1,000, the worker will usually be subject to larger deductions from his salary to help him to pay back at least part of the money owed, and he may be compelled by pressure from the boss to work more steadily. In no time in recent history was there ever any interest charged on loans by the bosses. The prospect would be considered an outrage by today's workers in much the same way as any curtailment of customary privileges was so considered in 1951. Most conscientious workers will manipulate the level of their debt to the boss so as to preserve their space in the division of labor, that is, to prevent the boss from firing them, and to prevent the debt from becoming so excessive as to make it impossible for the boss to collect by holding back wages of more than one month. Under such circumstances, pressure from the boss would most assuredly be felt.

There is, then, a definite boundary between availing one's self of protectionist privilege and owing one's soul to the company, and the large majority of workers do their best to steer clear of the latter condition, while recognizing that the former condition has advantages for them as well. The system of mutual control provided by the debt relationship and the means by which debt is manipulated in the interests of first one partner, then the other, is reminiscent of the debt relationships which Geertz described in a Javanese market, where debts are rarely settled permanently, and in which they form the basis of a lasting relationship between debtor and creditor (Geertz 1963a). Each partner uses other relationships in which his role may or may not be reversed to manipulate his debt to best advantage.

In the art-carved furniture industry, workers can count on a certain amount of credit from the boss to afford a minimal amount of economic protection from the forces of a free market for labor, on whose operation the workers are now more totally dependent in gaining their livelihood. That labor in this industry is still in short supply is probably one reason why today's workers have been able to preserve many of their protectionist privileges throughout the manufacturing period of the 1950s, as well as adding the contemporary privilege of command credit to the list.

One privilege which seems to have atrophied, however, with the boss's having assumed a role as a fount of credit, has been the traditional lunar New Year's bonus. Only 3% ($n = 290$) of workers questioned admitted to receiving a New Year's bonus. Today, New Year has rather become a time of heavy borrowing, when workers will go into debt for several hundred dollars to meet the many social obligations that arise during the vacation. Some workers will wish to borrow enough (H.K.$1,000) to return to their native villages to see relatives in China at this time. For those not lucky enough to return to China, or who dare not return, the vacation in Hong Kong will almost definitely involve some form of gambling during the New Year's holiday, when participation in games of chance is customary. The traditional New Year's bonus has been replaced for the most part by year-round interest-free loans, which intensify at New Year's time.

Nevertheless, on the evening of the last day before the New Year's holiday, the boss often throws a party for his workers, and beer and brandy flow freely.

Organization and relations of production

He and his workers converse more freely and for longer at the party than in all their combined conversations during the rest of the year. The food is plentiful and excellent. Apprentices sit at a separate table with the boss's children. All workers are invited, although not all of them come. Again, loyalty to the company is not a value of uppermost importance among the highly skilled workers. At least two workers at Heng Lung Co. who might have attended such a party had prior commitments that evening with their own families. Yet, the party is a gala occasion enjoyed by all who attend, and takes some of the formality out of the boss's relations with his workers. (For a description of New Year's festivities in a retail shop in East Central China see Fried 1953:81–2, 158.)

Nowadays, however, the trappings of protectionism involve credit more often than favors in kind, such as room and board or holiday dinners. Workers' loyalty has become a commodity purchased at a high price and stabilized with interest-free loans.

It has been suggested above that easily obtainable credit, as well as other forms of generosity, may be more freely dispensed by bosses who work alongside their workers, and that such practices also lend an air of informality to boss–worker relations. While accumulation has made the boss more than a first among equals, he preserves an aspect of this latter role in his relations with his carvers, who still own a portion (however small) of the means of production.

Carpenters' status has changed more significantly as the means of production have passed out of their hands, and this change is marked in the terms of present-day employment. Workers, particularly carpenters, are paid by the nine-hour working day or fraction thereof. While a greater prevalence of time- or day-wages was recorded in carpentry, carvers are also often found working for day-wages nowadays. The boss purchases his workers' labor power by the minute rather than by the number of pieces produced, although most workers still seem to prefer to work for piece-wages.

As I understand it, a factory in which workers are paid by the piece is a much calmer place to work. Workers are under much less pressure to produce. Their time is their own. As mentioned previously, they may work fast in the morning and take the afternoon off. They can also talk more freely during work hours. Working for day-wages, the boss is constantly on the alert to see that his workers are producing enough and that he is getting every productive ounce for every minute paid for. At Heng Lung Co. a day-wage carver was fired for working too slowly (p. 26). The worker promptly found another job at piecework rates where the pressure was not so great, although his pride suffered for a week or two after the incident.

Several workers told me that, generally speaking, day-wages favor the boss and are more exploitative of workers, whereas piecework tends to favor the workers. In a given historical period, like the present in Hong Kong, it is doubtful that piecework or timework actually express differing rates of labor exploitation.

The wood-carvers of Hong Kong

There are bosses who prefer to pay piecework because it means they can avoid the tension and aggravation of constantly having to oversee their workers. On the other hand, at the very least, day-wages usually assure the boss a more regular flow of output than stop-and-go piecework.

It may very well have been this demand for greater discipline that my worker friends were referring to when they linked day-wages with the interests of the boss. The preference for piece-wages may be an expression of resistance on the part of workers, accustomed to working at a self-determined pace to meet an accepted standard of living with piecework as the simple empirical measure of one's performance, to the demands for greater discipline from bosses of more highly capitalized production units. Every minute that the boss can keep his expensive capital equipment going means a gain in the productivity of his production unit. However, quite a number of workers expressed 'no preference' for either day- or piece-wages and it is likely that at this technological and organizational moment, the terms of one's employment do not reflect marked differences in the rate of labor exploitation.

The addition of power-driven machinery, nevertheless, was probably responsible for changing the nature of the work contract from piece- to time-wages, since it made the carpenter more than ever dependent on the sale of his labor at the boss's machines for his livelihood. Despite the fact that most bosses preserve a closeness with their workers by joining them in production and continuing to provide their workers with a variety of concessions, the work contract is now more characteristic of a proletarianized work organization.

Investment in power-driven carpentry machines and the greater productivity which they allow, led, as has been indicated in Chapter 1, to diversification into more modern styles, where that productivity could be more dramatically exploited. This has in turn fostered an increasing reliance on carpenters in production. In terms of the requirements of a unit of wooden furniture production, carpenters, despite their having assumed full proletarian status, are probably relatively more important than carvers who still own a portion of the means of production.

Moreover, carpentry in most contemporary production units is not yet totally mechanized. There is still a lot of careful shaping and hand preparation that goes on in the carpentry section of a carved-furniture establishment.

Many of these operations are still carried out with 'traditional' Chinese tools, as well as with western hand-tools, hammers, screwdrivers, plyers, chisels, etc. Many of the latter are of Japanese manufacture.

Among the traditional Chinese tools still employed are those where no significant increase in efficiency would be achieved by use of its western counterpart, or those to which a cultural preference outweighs any minimal advantages which might be gained.

A Chinese-style hardwood plane is an implement of the former type. There may well be operational advantages in its use over the steel planes of the west with which I am familiar. A factory requires an assortment of these planes in many different sizes and blade exposures, and these are all in constant use throughout the day at all factories. They consist of a simple block of hardwood, carved out to accommodate a steel plane blade with a wedge, one of which is illustrated in Hommel (1937:241, Fig. 354). The blade is placed in its slot and the wedge placed in on top. The wedge and the blade are then tapped alternately with a hammer until the desired blade exposure is attained. In the hands of a skilled carpenter, it is a precision shaping tool.

The Chinese-style bow saw, illustrated in Hommel (1937:231, Fig. 333), is also a commonly used tool. With steel saw blades, normally oriented at a 45° angle to the bow, the bow saw is no less efficient than the common western hand saw, and is preferred by Chinese carpenters long familiar with its use.

A present-day carpenter also employs a variety of templates for use in manufacturing various furniture parts identically, either with machines or by hand. Many of these templates are simple aids in the cutting out of regular circles, ovals and rectangles, but many are also outlines of traditional Chinese decorative lattice motifs, which have obviously come down from past ages of Chinese furniture manufacture since Ming times (1368–1644).

While it is unlikely that an individual carpenter nowadays will own enough of his own such tools to practice independent furniture manufacture, even excluding the need for power tools, the range in his expected wage is probably higher than that of his less fully proletarianized carving co-workers. This is partly because of the greater productivity which power-driven machines make possible, and partly because good carpenters have been in short supply in furniture factories since the 1960s when many took up work in the more lucrative construction industries.

In 1972–3, wages in both day and piecework varied from about H.K.$30 a day to H.K.$45 a day, for both carvers and carpenters. A boss at times requires the services of an extra carpenter when there is a large amount of merchandise which must be delivered on a particular date. For one or two days' service in such situations, a carpenter could be hired temporarily and paid as much as H.K.$55 a day. Normally, an experienced rough-carver or carpenter could make H.K.$45 a day or roughly $1,000 a month if he worked six days a week. The monthly wages reported by workers in 1973 are given in Table 2.

Wages for smooth-carvers generally run somewhat lower than for rough-carvers and carpenters, although a worker's skill and experience are the crucial determinants of his wage. Speed is also a consideration. A newly graduated apprentice carpenter earns about H.K.$30 a day. As a young journeyman, a worker continues to accumulate experience and the wages he is paid continue to increase. He may, if he is a carver, learn enough in his career to become a rough-carver; he also may not. After several years at a top salary, or after many years' experience in the industry, a *shifu*, or master, may be referred to and addressed as a *da shifu* (great master) or simply *da shi*. The term *huang di*

The wood-carvers of Hong Kong

Table 2. *Monthly wages reported by workers*

Monthly wage (H.K.$)	Number of workers		
300–500	5	} 16% less than	
501–700	41	H.K.$29/day	
701–900	88	} 59% between H.K.$29	} 84%
901–1,000	80	and 41/day	more than
1,001–1,200	40	} 25% more than	H.K.$29/
1,201–1,400	13	H.K.$41/day	day
1,400+	16		
	283 total		

(emperor or exalted one) is occasionally heard, less with respect to carpenters than to carvers, and very infrequently with respect to any carvers in Hong Kong. There are perhaps a handful of carvers who have been able to resist the trap of repetitious reproduction of the same basic motifs in the context of an industry whose expansion into the overseas market put a premium on speed and quantity rather than on quality, originality, versatility, expressiveness, etc. There are perhaps one or two carvers in all Hong Kong who merit designation as 'emperors'. Any Hong Kong carver whose skill came close to that of a true emperor would in any case deny his ability in deference to the great carvers still carving in Zhejiang, China, where production has not yet assumed so intensive a character as in Hong Kong (see Chapter 8).

Great master is also a term descriptive of a highly skilled carver or carpenter regardless of his relative wage at a given factory, and there are no accepted criteria, such as the production of a 'masterpiece' by which one achieves a given designation. It is conceivable that with respect to carving, prior to the incorporation of carvers into the production of furniture, the requirements of graduation for an apprentice included the production of such a work. It has, however, already been shown that nowadays the apprenticeship system rarely produces real 'masters' knowledgeable in all requirements of the craft, and the term 'master' today, for both carvers and carpenters, has as many gradations as cents in the dollar.

There are thus no hard and fast boundaries, rules or rites of passage at specific moments in one's career as a carver or carpenter when one earns a specific designation. Whatever hierarchy exists within a factory is a reflection of the money wages earned by the worker as representative of his relative skill and speed.

Painters

The painter's job is the dirtiest in the factory and allegedly for this reason he is often looked down upon by other workers as somehow less dignified. He is often isolated from the rest of the production workers in the retail portion of the business, and may seldom be seen by the carvers and carpenters in the course of the work day. I have seen carpenters and carvers deliberately sit at tables 'away from the painters' during lunch breaks. I am sure that painters' wages are not significantly lower than those of other workers, such as smooth-carvers, in the industry, and increased productivity in the industry throughout the 1960s must certainly have increased the demand for skilled painters, as well as increasing the wages they could command. Nevertheless, their status seems to have a caste-like quality to it which may go back some time in history.

In a strike which occurred in 1964, painters broke away from the striking carvers and carpenters and entered independent negotiations with employers (see Commissioner of Labor 1964–5:68–9), showing clearly that quite apart from political considerations of a communist versus non-communist nature, which had by 1964 all but obscured the craft boundaries of the manufacturing period, the synthetic structure of furniture manufacture was still manifest in real boundaries of interest between its separate craftsmen. The negative feelings of many workers towards painters as a group may have grown out of that period, but I have no direct evidence of this. What is more likely is that the almost outcaste painters in the mid-1960s entered independent negotiations with the employers for a better deal than they might have been able to secure in unified negotiations with carvers and carpenters among whom they were not respected.

Apart from the painters who employ stain and varnish, there are also those who paint designs on lacquered pieces, which are usually inlaid with stone, bone and shell. It is the job of such painters to paint in the background and setting of the scene depicted, and also to color appropriately the figures which are represented in inlaid materials. Many of these practitioners have had training in traditional Chinese brush painting and are respected as artists in a way that the stainer/varnisher is not. The lacquered wood which was traditionally employed in such work has now for the most part been replaced by plastic laminate. Inlays are now set into the plastic laminated wood. Where such inlay work and painting are required, they are usually subcontracted to a factory that specializes in such work, and that employs a group of full-time inlayers and painters, but such practitioners are not required for competitive production. They create the possibility of diversification into imitation lacquerware, but are marginal to carved-wood furniture production.

The stainer/varnisher, however, is a required practitioner who despite his usual isolation from carpenters and carvers remains indispensable to production.

Having thus completed this investigation of the capital and labor requirements of carved-wood furniture production, it should be clear that technical change manifested itself very differently in different niches of the manufacturing division of labor, and with the varying organizational and technical prerequisites of production in each niche. Production relations have changed, but with varying degrees of intensity in different niches as the labor and capital requirements of manufacture were undermined by the increased productivity of carpentry machines.

A change in the overall proportions of craft practitioners required in each niche of the division of labor was brought about by technical innovation, but a more diverse market affected the demand for the services of the various practitioners in a somewhat different direction.

The ideology of craft parochialism characteristic of manufacture has lingered on despite technological advance and increasing proletarianization of the labor force. This proletarianization itself was manifest in differing intensities in different niches of the division of labor, although terms of employment industry-wide came to reflect more closely the polarization brought about by accumulation of the modern means of production in capitalist hands.

A growing commercialization of boss—worker relations was also manifest in this context, although a certain informality and egalitarianism has persisted in these relations since many bosses, formerly workers themselves, continue to labor along with their workers.

4

Labor force composition and features

The labor force of the modern Hong Kong art-carved furniture industry has its origins primarily in the refugee populations which fled, or otherwise made their way, to Hong Kong during and immediately after the Chinese civil war of 1945–9, which ended in communist victory.

However, carved camphorwood chests were being produced in Hong Kong in 1940 just before the Japanese occupation of the colony in 1941. The *Directory and Chronicle of China, Japan, Straits Settlements and Malaya* listed ten camphorwood trunk establishments in the Crown Colony of Hong Kong in 1940 (five in Hong Kong, five in Kowloon). If, as has been suggested in Chapter 3, these units employed between 30 and 50 workers each, then the pre-war Hong Kong art-carved furniture workforce probably did not exceed 500 workers.

The influx of refugee carvers, carpenters and painters into Hong Kong during and following the civil war swelled the ranks of these workers. More than half of the workers interviewed on survey (54%) had entered the art-carved furniture workforce prior to 1951.

Apart from this first generation of refugees who had themselves worked in the furniture trades in China, a significant portion (29%) of today's labor force entered the trade between 1952 and 1961, an index of the industry's expansion in a regime of manufacture. In the thirty-two years from 1940 to 1972, the labor force of the Hong Kong art-carved furniture industry has witnessed a three to four-fold increase in numbers.

In the present-day labor force, workers fall into two categories when grouped according to their place of origin. There are workers from various parts of Guangdong province, the largest number coming from towns adjacent to Canton, where furniture production for export had its beginnings in the eighteenth century. Workers of Cantonese origin in the contemporary industry are fairly evenly drawn from the Shun De, Tai Shan, Kai Ping, San Shui, Xin Hui and Zhongshan districts of Guangdong province. The large majority of Hong Kong's contemporary population is of Cantonese origin and since the immediate post-1949 period, the majority of workers recruited into the art-carved furniture industry have been of Cantonese extraction, and of families with no prior connection to the furniture trades.

The most significant group of non-Cantonese refugees in the labor force in the immediate post-1949 period were those from Zhejiang province, most of whom had been associated with the export furniture industry centered around Shanghai. In pre-1949 Shanghai, it was the Zhejiang group who constituted the majority of workers in the art-carved furniture industry, both in its putting-out and 'manufacturing' phases.

Today one finds workers from the Ningbo, Hangzhou, Shaoxing, Jinhua and, most significantly, Dongyang counties of Zhejiang province scattered throughout the predominantly Cantonese labor force of the Hong Kong art-carved furniture industry.

Among Chinese working people, native place has always been an important determinant of social interaction. Shih Kuo-heng noted that workers formed groups in their factories according to their place of origin in wartime Yunnan (Shih 1944:9). Shanghainese workers in Kunming, during the Japanese occupation of eastern China, regularly sent money back to their relatives in and around Shanghai (Shih 1944:85). Such practices have always been common among Chinese emigrants far from their native villages (see Watson 1974). The political boundaries of occupied China in 1944 hampered, but could not stop, the flow of communications between relatives on both sides of the occupation line (Shih 1944:85).

In the art-carved furniture industry of today, almost 75% of workers of diverse places of origin (*n* = 229) still sent money back to relatives in their native villages in the communist-controlled mainland. This indicates that their native place still commands a significant loyalty among contemporary workers. The communist government on the mainland encourages the maintenance of such loyalties, so the political boundary between colonial Hong Kong and the communist mainland is regularly breached by this cash flow.

J. B. Tayler not only noted the existence of same native place groups in the labor force of the Hopei pottery industry, but also described marked cultural and behavioral characteristics of workers of differing native place.

The local T'angshan people [pottery workers] . . . are of a very thrifty, saving character; the Shantung potters known as the 'drinkers' from their addiction to alcohol; . . . the P'eng Ch'eng potters spent a good deal of money on display, being very particular about their clothes and fond of frequenting the theatres (Tayler 1930:202).

In contemporary Hong Kong, marked distinctions exist between workers of Zhejiang and Cantonese descent. The distinctive Wu dialects of Zhejiang refugees served in the early 1950s to mark them off as a group within the Hong Kong labor force quite apart from less obvious culture traits. A second generation of workers of Zhejiang origins has grown to maturity in Hong Kong, fluent in

Cantonese, and the linguistic boundary has tended to wane in significance, although other characteristics still distinguish the Zhejiang-derived group.

The demand for labor in the Hong Kong based art-carved furniture industry made it impossible for the Zhejiang workers to impose a monopoly on jobs in the teakwood and camphorwood industry for members of their own group (see p. 15). That this group was nevertheless of singular importance to the post-1949 development of the art-carved furniture industry in Hong Kong is revealed by the following sets of figures.

In Hong Kong today, Cantonese workers outnumber Zhejiang workers by a factor of almost five. 274 workers and apprentices reported a Cantonese place of origin and only 58 workers and apprentices reported a Zhejiang place of origin. However, with respect to shop and factory proprietors, Cantonese bosses outnumbered Zhejiang bosses by a factor of less than two. There were 44 shop and factory bosses of Cantonese origin and 28 shop and factory bosses of Zhejiang origins in the sample. In the art-carved furniture industry in which a boss and perhaps a partner are the sole shareholders, this is a clear indication of the provenience of a good deal of the capital for the post-war development of the wood-carving industry, and indicates the importance of the capital contribution of the Zhejiang refugee group to that development.

Apart from this disproportionate number of bosses, there are several other distinctive attributes which stand out in the Zhejiang workers group. Zhejiang workers claim to have a superior carving and carpentry skill (p. 15). While this is a difficult claim to substantiate in an objective fashion, in my own experience the knowledge that a worker, particularly a carver, was of Zhejiang background created the expectation for me that his skill would be of a high calibre and the expectation was usually confirmed. There are also many highly skilled Cantonese workers in the industry today, but the proportion of *da shifu* (great masters) among Cantonese workers is probably not as high as among their fellow workers of Zhejiang origin. Quality carved products exported from Mainland China to this day come from Zhejiang province, with cheaper export goods, less elaborately executed, produced in Canton.

One possible factor which might account for the Zhejiang group's having been able to preserve this superior skill in the Hong Kong setting in spite of the fact that they could not completely monopolize jobs in the art-carved furniture industry in the post-war period, was their ability to keep their skills within the family, teaching their sons and family members the tricks they had learned through long association with the trade in Shanghai. Of a total of 404 workers, bosses and apprentices interviewed, 110, or only 27.2%, had followed their fathers into the art-carved furniture trade.

As shown in Table 3, of these 110 workers, bosses and apprentices, 38 were of Zhejiang extraction, which represented 44.1% of the total of 86 workers, bosses and apprentices of Zhejiang origins. 72 of the 110 workers, bosses and apprentices were of Cantonese origin, which, however, represented only

The wood-carvers of Hong Kong

Table 3. *Correlation of native place with incidence of following one's father into the art-carved furniture trade*

	Zhejiang	Guangdong	Total
Father in the profession	38 (44.1%)	72 (22.6%)	110
Father not in the profession	48 (55.9%)	246 (77.4%)	294
Total	86	318	404

22.6% of the total of 318 workers, bosses and apprentices from Guangdong in the sample.

Thus, in spite of the fact that the post-war market for art-carved furniture was big enough to sustain the entrance into the labor force of a large number of workers unrelated to previous generations of workers, the profession and its skills continue to be passed down from father to son with greatest frequency among Zhejiang workers.* This may very well contribute to the perpetuation of a Zhejiang aristocracy of skill in the labor force, membership of which is restricted by the bounds of kinship, and also to some extent *de facto* by place of origin.

Carving families are generally of more common occurrence among Zhejiang workers. K.W. Ng, a 27-year-old Zhejiang carver with Dongyang county antecedents, has a younger brother learning the trade from him. Their father, now deceased, was a carver with pre-war experience in Shanghai. Their eldest brother is still in Shanghai working as a furniture-producing carpenter, and various paternal uncles and cousins are scattered throughout Hong Kong's art-carved furniture factories practising either carving or carpentry.

A total of 80 workers listed relatives other than their fathers who were engaged in the art-carved furniture industry. They listed a total of 11 uncles, 38 brothers, 11 cousins, 8 sons and 1 grandson. A further measure of the relative importance of kinship in recruitment among Zhejiang workers is evidenced by the fact that of the 80 workers who listed such relatives, 20 were of Zhejiang extraction, out of a total of 45 Zhejiang *workers* in the sample, while 60 were of Cantonese extraction, of a total of 240 Cantonese workers in the sample. The rate of occurrence of relatives in the same trade for Zhejiang workers is hence 4 for every 9, or almost 1 for every 2, while the rate for Cantonese is only 1 for every 4 workers.

The most common occupation of workers' fathers who were *not* engaged in art-carved furniture production was, as might be expected, that of peasant

* For an interesting discussion of another profession (butchers) in which conditions allowed restriction of outsiders from the profession, see Hsü and Ho (1945).

farmer (*nong min*). 12 of the 45 Zhejiang workers in the sample (roughly 27%), and 86 of 240 Cantonese workers in the sample (roughly 36%), listed their father's occupation as peasant farmer. The higher percentage of Cantonese workers recruited from peasant families is consistent with the lower frequencies with which Cantonese workers followed their fathers or other relatives into the wood-carving trade.

Thus the Zhejiang workers in today's industry are distinguished by a greater likelihood of having followed their fathers or other relatives into the trade, and a greater tendency to pass the trade on to their descendants. This normally means that a Zhejiang worker's family has had a longer association with the wood-carving profession and may very likely be reflected in the superior skill of workers of Zhejiang origin.

Probably as a result of these same characteristics, the Zhejiang carver is usually more familiar with a wider range of traditional motifs and the traditional stories which they represent. These motifs were, and still tend to be, derived from events depicted in the *San Guo Zhi* (Annals of the Three Kingdoms), a compilation of histories of the period A.D.222–65. These histories describe the exploits of the leaders of the states of Shu, Wei and Wu, states which came into existence with the decline of the later Han dynasty. Their representation in temple carvings similar to those incorporated into the furniture of post-1895 Shanghai dates at least from Tang times (Stanley 1914:78). Since 1949 and the enormous expansion of the production of carved-wood products in Hong Kong for export to western countries, the reproduction of such motifs and stories was replaced by more extemporaneous freehand carving, in which the depiction of actual historical figures was no longer of any great significance. As a result, a generation of apprentices has been raised through the ranks without really learning the culture associated with the motifs they learned to reproduce. Among Zhejiang workers, where family association with the carving profession is likely to have been longer, and where it is more likely that a boy will be learning the profession from someone with whom he is related, it is probable that during the apprenticeship period he will become more familiar with the traditional motifs and the particular attributes of their characters than his Cantonese fellow worker. In my own experience, it was workers of Zhejiang origins who showed greater familiarity with the histories and stories behind the motifs that they carved.

Of the Zhejiang workers in the art-carved furniture industry, more than half came from the county (*xian*) of Dongyang, as did my boss at Heng Lung Co. Everything said thus far about Zhejiang workers applies with even greater force to workers from Dongyang county. The most highly skilled workers in today's industry, the one or two workers who might qualify as *huang di* (emperors), are, without exception, of Dongyang ancestry. Dongyang county was one of the areas to which work was first contracted out by urban-based Shanghai furniture firms, and its inhabitants constituted a significant percentage of the workforce in the early years of furniture 'manufacture' in Shanghai.

Older Dongyang workers, with work experience in the setting of Shanghai based art-carved furniture manufacture, however, were never able to state clearly why Dongyang, as opposed to any other place in Zhejiang province, should have developed such early or extensive ties with the Shanghai-centered trade, or why Dongyang should have produced so many and such fine craftsmen. This remains somewhat of a mystery, the solution of which can only be deduced from fragmentary evidence.

Dongyang is a poor, rural, hilly region of east-central Zhejiang and lies at the apex of a roughly equilateral triangle on the map, with Ningbo and Hangzhou at the other corners. According to the Zhejiang *Industrial Handbook* of 1932, it lay in the Hangzhou economic district whose towns and villages ranked first in Zhejiang province in terms of their volume of trade with Shanghai (Ho 1935:97).

The prime agricultural product of Dongyang county was, and is, pigs, of which its production was the largest in the province in 1932: 170,000 pigs valued at H.K.$3,400,000. The pigs did not constitute a great source of external commercial ties, as only 1,000 of them found their way to market in Hangzhou in 1932 (Ho 1935:380-1).

According to the *Handbook*, soil in districts like Dongyang 'consists principally of sandy loam, which needs frequent and generous fertilization, hence *pigs are raised* almost in every farm *to provide manure* for the fields as well as for stock purposes' (Ho 1935:614, emphasis added).

Dongyang was a rice-deficient area, producing some 42% less than its actual needs of over 1,700,000 piculs in 1932. Nevertheless, it stood first in the production of maize in the province of Zhejiang, where, according to the *Handbook,* the majority of the rural population subsists mainly on maize flour. Zhejiang was in 1932 a rice-deficient province. All of Dongyang's maize was consumed locally which made it roughly 84% self-sufficient in grain, probably not an altogether bad figure for Zhejiang in 1932.

Dongyang led the province in the production of peaches in 1932 with 30,000 piculs. Among its other agricultural products were chestnuts, dates, lotus root, feitzu nuts, cabbage, bamboo shoots, turnips and taro, sweet potato, rapeseed and tea, almost all of which, with the exception of tea, were consumed locally. Barley was also grown, largely for animal feed, and, in this livestock area, barley fetched the highest price per picul in the province in 1932.

Land is generally of poor quality and the price for first-grade agricultural land was the highest in the province in 1932. Lesser grades of land were, however, substantially cheaper. Probably as a consequence of this, the average family holding in Dongyang was the highest in the province, 133.2 mou per family, a very high figure for rural China at this time. As mentioned above, the demand for fertilizer on large tracts of this poor land was great, and was supplied by pig raising.

Among its industrial endeavors were hosiery knitting, cord and thread production, pottery and soap manufacture and some silk weaving. The knitting and thread industries were organized almost entirely as cottage industries, work being done in farmers' homes in the agricultural off-season or in free moments by household members. Merchant employers based in Shanghai or Hangzhou collected the finished goods and marketed them outside the county.

There is little hint in any of the foregoing as to what might distinguish Dongyang county as a center of skilled woodworkers. The *Zhejiang Industrial Handbook* furthermore only lists woodcarving and furniture producing firms in the larger cities and towns of Zhejiang — Hangzhou, Ningbo, Shaoxing and Lanji.

As has been stated, Dongyang county, although grouped in the Hangzhou economic district of Zhejiang, lay roughly equidistant from both Hangzhou and Ningbo. This suggests that traditional economic ties with Ningbo may also have been extensive, a fact which may help to explain how Dongyang workers were able to establish the dominant position they later came to occupy in the Shanghai art-carved furniture industry. Among the traditional carved items which Sowerby lists as providing carvings for the furniture manufacturers catering to the carved-furniture craze at the turn of the century, apart from temple carvings and shop-front decorations, were the 'well known Ningbo beds' (Sowerby 1926:2). Shiba (1977:412) mentions such beds as among those products whose component parts were produced in a putting-out system. Sowerby's 1926 article has a plate (facing p. 3) illustrating a set of carved-wood screens whose carved panels had been removed from such a bed and built into the newly constructed screen frame.

Ningbo was a traditional center of paint and varnish production, and in 1932 had thirty-seven concerns producing art-carved furniture (Ho 1932:123-4). Traditionally it was also a key collection, distribution and trans-shipment point along the entire east coast for many raw materials, including lumber and exotic woods (Shiba 1977:396, 399). By 1932, much of the lumber for furniture manufacture in Ningbo was imported through Shanghai, but, in the traditional context, this lumber came largely from Anhui and eastern Zhejiang (*Handbook* 1932:737).

Dongyang was classified, in 1932, as belonging to the second forestation section of Zhejiang province, which produced both camphor trees and various species of *dalbergia*, the former in great demand in the lacquered campaign chests very popular in the nineteenth century, and the latter being a species of rosewood favored by Chinese furniture producers since the eighth century (Ecke 1944:22-3). Dongyang was noted as one of the places in eastern Zhejiang where supplies of furniture wood and subsidiary supplies (probably camphorwood) for the production of lacquerware could be obtained. It is probable that the rural temple carvers of Dongyang county had been involved in the production of carvings for items of furniture and lacquerware, such Ningbo beds and wooden chests, prior to the opening of the port in Shanghai. Several Dongyang carvers in today's workforce attest to the fact that Dongyang had a few well-known carvers in earlier times. Furthermore, among my Dongyang informants, several had had work experience in Ningbo and Hangzhou as well as Shanghai.

As Dongyang was an area traditionally known for its lumber, it seems probable that it supplied the traditional paint and varnish center of Ningbo with skilled workers in wood, conceivably in a putting-out framework (Shiba 1977:411–12). Prior to the opening of an overseas market, employment in such coastal industries or in carving temples was probably limited and intermittent. The increased demand for carvings which ensued in Shanghai in the post-1985 period, put a premium on the talents of the skilled wood-workers of Dongyang county. Once the residents of Dongyang had a hold on jobs in the expanding Shanghai furniture trade, it is likely that they tended to take apprentices from their native villages, either children of kin or children of associates and friends. This practice is consistent with what is known of Chinese craftsmen in traditional times, and, as has been pointed out, survives to some extent even today. The depth of involvement of Dongyang county residents in the woodcarving and furniture trades is confirmed today by the fact that there is at present a substantial wood-carving and furniture manufacturing industry of some 1,000 workers operating out of Dongyang county itself, producing carved furniture for export direct from the Peoples' Republic. Anyone who has ever seen any of the products of the modern Dongyang-centered industry on sale in China products stores of Hong Kong can easily recognize the characteristic delicacy and elegance of their execution. Their quality is far superior to anything turned out in contemporary Hong Kong, even by craftsmen of Dongyang ancestry.

Present-day Hong Kong residents of Dongyang descent still constitute a rather tight-knit social group within the art-carved furniture workforce. Friendships and family ties from the old country are still strong among workers and even between bosses and workers, and are preserved in the Dongyang *tong xiang hui* (same native place association). There are some 250 member families in the association, almost 90% of whom are in one way or another associated with the art-carved furniture industry. The association has been in existence in Hong Kong since 1923, but was formally incorporated with the purchase of a flat which served as its headquarters in 1973. My boss, Mr Li, of Heng Lung Co. was a founding member of the newly incorporated association, and contributed H.K.$1,000 toward the purchase of the flat. His name appears, together with those of the other founding members and the amounts contributed by each, engraved in a stone plaque set into the wall of the headquarters.

The association is not a large one and its sources of funds for carrying out welfare activities are not great. Nevertheless, every Sunday twenty to thirty members go up to the headquarters to play mah-jong, and the headquarters is occasionally rented to members for parties. At times the association sponsors outings to the New Territories, and pictures of past outings decorate a portion of one of the walls in the headquarters. Most important among its functions is the provision of a sum of money to the families of deceased members for funeral expenses.

Membership of the association cuts across class lines although members are for the most part shop and factory proprietors. Only ten workers interviewed during the survey had ever participated in the activities of a same native place association. Since membership of such associations was traditionally reserved for citizens of substance (Van der Sprenkle 1962:91), and since the ordinary worker was seldom of sufficient means, this statistic is not particularly surprising. However, of the ten workers in the sample of today's workforce who were participants, five were members of the Dongyang same native place association, which does give some indication of the relative importance of this association among workers in the art-carved furniture industry. In addition, it should be noted that the Dongyang association maintained a category of 'ordinary individual membership', obtainable at a quite nominal fee, so it is possible that larger numbers of worker members remained undetected by the survey.

Increasingly, Dongyang natives have taken advantage of the relaxation in the Communist Chinese diplomatic stance toward Hong Kong residents, and many have travelled back to their native villages. My boss at Heng Lung Co. made the trip in 1973, together with his wife, for the first time in more than twenty-five years. Having left their native village before the Chinese civil war, they were not politically suspect, but neither were they supporters in any way of communist ideology or practice.

The tendency noted by Shih (1944:11) and Tayler (1930:202) for workers to associate and form groups with fellow provincials and for these groups to possess and maintain certain marked cultural characteristics, has thus persisted into the contemporary Hong Kong art-carved furniture industry, and this tendency may become increasingly marked in the recruiting of carvers, as the number of positions in the labor force for carvers falls off (p. 31). With the industry diversifying further into modern styles in which carving is of less significance, it is conceivable that native place may very well become increasingly important in restricting the recruitment of carvers into the industry as the number of available positions becomes more limited.

Nevertheless, Zhejiang and Cantonese workers have been working side by side for more than thirty years in the Hong Kong based industry (p. 15). The linguistic boundary which defined such groups so clearly in the early 1950s has atrophied. But, more important, the interests of particularist solidarity in this industry have at present given way to a large extent to those of class solidarity, which have become increasingly dominant as the industry has expanded through the late 1950s and 1960s.

While workers may still establish friendships and maintain relationships with greater ease among their fellow provincials, there exists a genuine feeling of cameraderie and community among workers in the industry, based on a perception of their common interests as art-carved furniture workers. This occupational community is one in which there is often a close face-to-face relationship between large numbers of fellow workers, regardless of their place of origin.

In Chapter 1, mention was made of the rather high mobility rate of workers between firms within the art-carved furniture industry and this was attributed to a shortage of labor in a free labor market, in which workers have little protection or security beyond the price of their labor power. It is this rather high mobility rate that contributes to and sustains the widespread and close relations between large numbers of fellow art-carved furniture workers and to a certain extent mitigates the effects of same native place as a determinant of workers' social interactions centered in the work place.

After seven months' work at Heng Lung Co., it was clear that every factory in the industry was a nodal point in a complex industry-wide network of communications and gossip, along the lines of which personnel and information travelled on a regular basis. After seven months at Heng Lung Co., only four out of fifteen workers originally employed there, or who had been hired during the period, remained on the job. Six carvers left, two carpenters left (one of them came back and left again) and two apprentices left to take up work at other factories. From time to time, workers who had worked at Heng Lung Co. before my arrival would show up to renew acquaintances with old friends there and share the latest gossip and news. Workers at Heng Lung would also often take afternoons off to visit friends at other factories with whom they had worked in the past. By accompanying workers at Heng Lung Co. on such afternoon outings it was possible to get a good look at large numbers of art-carved furniture factories throughout the colony of Hong Kong, and to meet and talk to large numbers of workers at each of these factories.

Word travels fast along these channels and news of all kinds is constantly brought along on such visits. Often when I appeared for the first time at a factory with my survey crew, workers would already have heard by word of mouth of my existence as an apprentice at Heng Lung Co. Information of a more important nature is also exchanged, and helps a worker keep abreast of developments throughout the industry which may concern his livelihood.

Hey, How are you? Are you still working at —— Co.? Is —— still working there? I used to work with him at —— Co. Hey, let me introduce you to —— here. We used to work together at —— Co. You remember ——? He moved over to ——'s factory on —— Road. You say —— Co. needs workers? Hmm, you know I'd consider working down there, but he'd have to pay me better than I'm paid here, and it's so damn far from my home in ——. Yeah, you let me know if you hear anything more about it.

is a summary of the kind of information invariably exchanged on such visits.

Labor force composition and features

A worker's friends and fellow workers were the overwhelmingly most common source of information concerning available jobs. As a worker moves from factory to factory in the course of his career, he becomes acquainted with ever larger numbers of his fellow workers, and the communications network from which he may garner information concerning the industry as a whole or possibilities of future employment grows more complex.

In the course of administering the survey, each worker was asked how long he had been at his current place of work, and was further requested to specify his previous five places of employment and the duration of each. Adding together the length of the reported period of work for each factory and dividing by the total number of factories gave a rough average of the duration of stay per factory of each worker, and hence a rough measure of labor mobility.

The results in Table 4 can be conveniently divided into four groups of differing mobility rates. There is a very high mobility group, which constituted 13% (34) of the workers responding, who spent an average of less than one year in any factory; a high mobility group of 14% (36) of the workers, who spent an average of between one and two years; a middle mobility group of 42% (110) of the workers who spent an average of between two and five years; and a low mobility group of 30% (77) of the workers who spent an average of more than five years.

The results show a pattern slightly more stable than the rate of labor turnover at Heng Lung Co. might have suggested, but indicate clearly that there is scarcely any vestige in present-day Hong Kong of the almost ritualized company solidarity of traditional Chinese craftsmen (Fried 1953:82).

High labor mobility is almost certainly a result of labor scarcity. In 1972–3 workers could almost always find work to do in the industry at wages comparable to or better than their current place of employment. In the survey, workers were asked first to account for labor mobility as a phenomenon industry-wide, and then to state why in each instance they had left the factories specified in their own work histories. Table 5 indicates the variety and number of responses of workers in accounting for mobility in an objective sense, and workers' own stated reasons for leaving particular factories.

The most frequent response in both cases was the worker's search for a better wage, which confirms the assumption that workers move from job to job in a labor-scarce market taking best advantage of the situation to sell their labor to the highest bidder. 'Finding more work to do'* may also be interpreted along these lines as an attempt by the worker to maintain or improve his monthly

---

* Finding more work to do is often a euphemism for having been fired, since bosses often let a worker know he is through at a given factory by claiming there are insufficient orders to provide him with work whether there are insufficient orders or not. It is also conceivable that there are many small firms who operate with a fluctuating number of workers as the number of their orders rise and fall in the normal course of their operation. There was some evidence of this at Heng Lung Co.

63

The wood-carvers of Hong Kong

Table 4. *Labor force mobility*

Total years	Number of factories						Mobility
	1	2	3	4	5	6	
1	0						Very high
2	0	5	7				mobility,
3				8			less than
4	6				8	6	1 year/factory,
5			6				34 workers
6				5			13%+
7							High mobility
8		15		8			
9						13	1–2 years/factory,
10							36 workers
11			27				14%
12							
13							
14				18			
15							Middle mobility,
16	26						
17					21		2–5 years/factory,
18							
19							110 workers
20		21				23	42%+
21							
22			15				
23							
24							
25							
26				11			
27							
28							
29					0		
30+							
						3	Low mobility, 5+ years/factory, 77 workers 30%

Labor force composition and features

Table 5. *Workers' responses in accounting for labor mobility*

Objectively	
The search for better wages	157
Finding more work to do	130
The desire to change one's work environment or working conditions	53
Conflicts or dissatisfaction with boss	46
The desire to gain more experience	4
Personal reasons	2
Depends on business	2
Personally	
To get a better wage	122
To find more work to do	101
To seek better working conditions	37
Conflict with the boss	38
To get experience	24
Asked by another boss	8
To work with friends	3
Graduated apprenticeship	2
Followed master	2
Father started a furniture business	1

wage, where he can, by following the fluctuating fortunes of various firms throughout the industry.

Also of note was the simple desire to change one's work environment. Many workers enjoy a move simply because it gives them an opportunity to work in another part of town, or in a factory with a looser or tighter work organization or pace, and will change factories in accordance with their immediate preferences. Working with friends or for a different and more understanding boss, or simply to gain a wider experience of the industry, were significant responses.

These options are usually open to a worker in this labor-scarce industry. The greatest concentration of the responses, recorded in Table 4, of duration of stay per factory was in the '6—10 years at 3 different factories' range or a modal stay of 2 to 3 years per factory per worker, after which a change of work place for one reason or another ensued.

Bosses often go to great lengths to ensure a stable labor supply, and having workers in debt is one means by which the boss can attempt to cut down his workers' freedom of movement (p. 45). A total of 141 workers gave figures for the most they had ever been in debt to their bosses *and* figures for their mobility patterns (see Table 6). While a significant number of workers in the very high and high mobility groups was still able to move fairly freely, despite accrued debts to the boss of over H.K.$1,000, the table shows a shifting of the balance of mobility from moderate—high to moderate—low as the level of debt rises above H.K.$1,000:

Table 6. *Debt and mobility*

Mobility	H.K.$1–499	H.K.$500–999	H.K.$1,000+	Total
Very high	7	4	4	15
High	19	7	8	34
Moderate	25	7	15	47
Low	16	12	17	45
Total	67	30	44	141

This is a high price to secure the labor power of one worker, and an inadequate one in many instances. Labor scarcity is such that this price is often equalled in the form of loans by other bosses competing for labor, and, as can be seen from Table 6, *was* equalled in at least twelve cases of workers with high and very high mobility rates and debts of H.K.$1,000 or more. Debts of less than H.K. $500 seem to have little effect on a worker's freedom of movement.

The high labor mobility in the industry and the extensive communications network throughout the industry, which it both helps to maintain and is maintained by, contributes to a sense of community among workers as workers. The focus of their loyalty is not toward the firm, and less toward their fellow provincials than toward their fellow workers as a group, and toward getting the most for their labor.

It was probably the prevalence of such conditions in the workforce that fitted the workers so well for unionization, which became increasingly important to their well-being as they became progressively more alienated from the means of production in the 1960s.

5

Unionism

The background

The origin of independent Chinese workers' organizations is rooted in the dissolution of traditional Chinese guilds which dates from the Republican period (1911–49), if not somewhat earlier. The process of guild breakdown was often linked to the opening of export markets beyond the control of the guilds, the increasing inability of the guilds to control the actions of their members, and, in this context, the undermining of their power to maintain monopolistic practices like price fixing (Fong 1929; Ch'u and Blaisdell 1924). This process was probably more advanced in South China where Sun Yat-sen's Guomindang party, still in alliance with the Chinese Communist party in the early 1920s, was actively engaged in organizing unions of a modern type among craftsmen and industrial workers. Burgess noted that out of 180 unions surveyed by the city government of Canton in 1927, 74 were former guilds that had been reorganized (Burgess 1928:225). The *Chun Wah* Union of workers in rosewood, which is still operating in contemporary Hong Kong and which was organized in Canton in 1922 was probably of this type.

The process of union organization was also well advanced in Shanghai by the late 1920s. A strike of wooden trunk workers (probably carved camphorwood chest workers) was recorded in the *Chinese Economic Journal* (1927b:1:3:232) for the year 1926, as having been the longest of the year. Workers with work experience in Shanghai in the present-day Hong Kong workforce mentioned a wood-carvers' or furniture-workers' union as having existed in Shanghai in the late pre-war period and in whose activities they participated.

In Hangzhou, however, the process of guild dissolution had yet to run its course by 1927 in the wood-carving industries where both workers and shop owners still shared membership in a common guild (*Chinese Economic Journal* 1927b:1:2:223).

Pre-war Hong Kong, where a small number of carved-wood items were produced, does not seem to have had a genuine workers' organization of constituent craftsmen. A union of sorts, called the *Chit-Yuet* (Zhejiang-Guangdong)

The wood-carvers of Hong Kong

Camphorwood Chest Workers' Guild came into existence in about 1945. It does not seem to have been a true guild in the sense that it represented both labor and capital, nor does it seem to have been a true union or employer's association. Its membership consisted largely of factory foremen, perhaps labor contractors, described by left-wing workers today as a class of small bourgeoisie who wavered in allegiance between the workers and bosses.

In the period just prior to 1949, the foremen's 'guild' is said to have put pressure on factory bosses to maintain the level of workers' real wages in the face of severe inflation. The guild collapsed shortly before 1949, and, while it is said that there are still a few of its members around in the industry, it was never my good fortune to meet one, or to know about it if I did.

In any event, the legacy of the traditional pattern of craft organization, which was manifest in the existence of guilds, persisted in the structure of the labor force of the art-carved furniture industry in the period of manufacture of the 1950s, and manifested itself in the variety of trade unions which came into existence at that time. Traditional boundaries between carpenter and carver, between rosewood and teak/camphorwood workers, and between craftsmen of different places of origin were all manifest in separate organizations of craft practitioners in the early 1950s and remained strong throughout the period of manufacture. Five unions thrived in this period, three in the teak/camphorwood industry, with which I am here primarily concerned, and two in rosewood.

After World War II unionism in the Hong Kong based art-carved furniture industry saw traditional craft parochialism become manifest in a politically based polarization of the industry along communist—nationalist lines, as the mode of production of art-carved furniture became transformed from labor-intensive craft manufacture to capital-intensive, fully proletarianized industrial production. In this context, the communist Hong Kong—Kowloon Woodwork Carvers' Union emerged as the dominant group in the labor force. It did so by adapting its proletarian message in various ways to the local conditions of its existence, while these conditions themselves underwent change, giving greater cogency to that message.

The nationalist—communist political division came into play very early in the history of Chinese unionism. As early as 1925, the expulsion by the Guomindang-sponsored General Federation of Labor of its pro-communist members led to the establishment of the rival Labor Union Representative Federation of left-wing persuasion (Lockwood 1927:399). The existence of competing labor factions represented by groups like the Nationalist Trade Union Council and the Communist Federation of Trade Unions of post-war Hong Kong is only the latter-day expression of this early split in the Chinese labor movement. In post-war Hong Kong it was not unusual to find competing unions within the same industry, affiliated with each of these umbrella organizations, and the art-carved furniture industry was no exception.

The organization of a 'carpenters'' union in 1951 of nationalist persuasion

68

had brought into existence in the following year, first, a 'carvers'' union of communist persuasion, and then a union of carvers from Zhejiang/Shanghai of nationalist persuasion.

The carpenters' union (the Camphorwood Trunk Workers' Union) is still in existence but has not fared well. Its membership has been declining since 1962, and in 1976 it claimed a registered membership of only fourteen members. It is affiliated with the nationalist Trade Union Council whose power has waned considerably since the expulsion from the United Nations in 1971 of the Nationalist government on Taiwan.

The carvers' union of communist persuasion (the Woodwork Carvers' Union) has prospered. In 1971 it boasted a membership of 508 workers and a vigorous recruitment drive was underway when I left Hong Kong at the end of 1973, which resulted in an almost 50% increase in membership by 1977. It is associated with the communist Federation of Trade Unions.

The carvers' union of workers from Zhejiang/Shanghai of nationalist persuasion (the Artistic Woodworkers' Union) was first organized in 1952 and was active in strike action in 1964, but seems to have passed out of active existence. Its membership has not changed significantly since 1966, and, never having encountered a worker who claimed membership in this union, I believe it may have become defunct. It is not uncommon in Hong Kong for such organizations to maintain their names on official books even though they have long since ceased to function. I believe the assimilation into the Hong Kong melting pot of a second generation of carvers and carpenters of Zhejiang/Shanghai origins, born in Hong Kong and fluent in Cantonese, may have seriously undermined much of the basis for its existence independent of the nationalist carpenters' union. An unspecified portion of its functional *raison d'être* may have been absorbed by the Dongyang same native place association.

The extremely sharp distinction which existed in the early 1950s between workers in teak/camphorwood and those in rosewood has lost its currency today. In recent years, the demand for teak/camphorwood products has declined, brought about largely by the decreasing purchasing power abroad of the American dollar, and the increasing value of the Japanese *yen*. The Japanese preference for products of rosewood has created a situation in which many workers in the Woodwork Carvers' Union who had previously never worked in anything but teak/camphorwood, have begun to take up rosewood carving for the first time in rather large numbers. The influence of the Woodwork Carvers' Union among rosewood workers has grown in proportion to that change, and in 1973 there were discussions in progress about the possibility of amalgamating the two left-wing unions, with the Rosewood Workers' Union being the junior partner in numbers (see Table 7).*

Figures for membership in teak/camphorwood unions until 1977, compiled from the Hong Kong government Registry of Trade Unions, are given in Table 8.

* This amalgamation had still not occurred when I returned to Hong Kong in 1978.

The wood-carvers of Hong Kong

Table 7. *Variety of unions*

	Communist		Nationalist	
	Carpenter	Carver	Carpenter	Carver
Teak/ camphorwood		Hong Kong– Kowloon Woodwork Carvers' Union	Camphorwood Trunk Workers' Union	Zhejiang/ Shanghai
				Artistic Wood- workers' Union
Rosewood	Rosewood Workers' Union		Chun Wah Union (founded 1922)	

It is clear from these figures how the fortunes of each of the unions are linked to international political developments. Membership in the pro-nationalist Taiwan unions outnumbered membership in the pro-communist Mainland union in only four years since 1953, three of which, 1962, 1962 and 1964, immediately followed the 'three bad years' on the Mainland. Setbacks in the years following the Great Leap Forward were well reported in Hong Kong by many who fled to the colony at that time. Only by 1966 did pro-communist union membership again surpass the combined pro-nationalist figures. Only since 1971 and the aftermath of the Cultural Revolution in China and the international recognition of the Peking government at the United Nations has the Woodwork Carvers' Union been able truly to consolidate its hold.

In post-war Hong Kong, trade unionism has generally been weak. In the industrial sector, union membership averages only 6.5% of the total labor force (England 1971:237–8). There is a greater concentration of union membership in the public utilities and communications sector, in which the communist trade union movement made a concerted organizing effort just after 1949 to consolidate a Mainland Chinese stake in the future of Hong Kong. In these two areas, 64.3% and 53.1% of the workers respectively are trade union members (England 1971:238).

Among the other areas of high percentages of union membership are certain industries in the so-called 'traditional sector', where old guild traditions of collective bargaining are said to exist (England 1971:248). The high percentages of union membership in the art-carved furniture industry, in the 50–60% range in 1960, and rising back up to and beyond that level today, might well be taken to represent continuity with guild precedents set in places like Hangzhou in the late 1920s, well within the lifetime and experience of refugee artisans in Hong Kong in the 1950s, and even of some of today's workers. However, this

Table 8. *Membership figures in teak/camphorwood unions*

	Camphorwood trunk workers	Artistic woodworkers	Woodwork carvers
1949			
1950			
1951	195		
1952			
1953	192	133	299
1954			
1955	165	160	426
1956	128	156	443
1957	194	130	455
1958	191	133	494
1959	212	135	492
1960	238	136	516
1961	246	137	490
1962	245	138	202
1963	223	138	217
1964	175	138	246
1965	146	138	237
1966	134	61	243
1967	131	61	252
1968	130	61	270
1969	136	61	311
1970	132	61	471
1971	82	61	508
1972	79	61	541
1973	58	61	684
1974	58	60	715
1975	14	60	740
1976	14	60	743
1977	21	60	805

artisan group, many of whose members had work experience in Canton and Shanghai, were no strangers to unionism. According to Ch'u Teh this artisan class was politically 'enlightened, independent and alert' and constituted 'the advanced guard of the later (Chinese) industrial proletariat' (Smedley 1974:23). Intractable, yet indispensable to production, this workforce also brought to Hong Kong a tradition of union activity built upon and already beginning to alter the social structure of guild organization.

In the Hong Kong of the 1950s, labor was in short supply, mobility between firms was high and good communications networks existed throughout the art-carved furniture industry. While political divisions and the regulations of the Hong Kong government made the imposition of closed shop regulations an impossibility, labor scarcity, high mobility and good communications within the labor force of highly intractable skilled workers must have provided a setting quite conducive to union organizing, and to the perpetuation of whatever remained of guild-like collective bargaining in slightly redressed form.

The strikes

The first post-war strike in the Hong Kong art-carved furniture industry is recorded in the Annual Report of the Commissioner of Labor for the year 1951 (Commissioner of Labor 1951–2:33–5). It was this strike which accounted for the formation of the Camphorwood Trunk Workers' Union (nationalist, carpenters), and was mentioned in Chapter 3 in connection with workers defending their customary privileges of gambling and sleeping in the factories of their employ.

The strike arose initially over a disagreement on piecework rates, and discontent over measures taken to suppress gambling at George Zee & Co., to this day one of the larger firms in the Hong Kong art-carved furniture industry, and a company which had been one of the major producers of carved-wood furniture in Shanghai prior to 1949, with a shop on fashionable Nanking Road.

It was a foreman who encouraged the workers to leave work and some 60 out of 100 did. He may have been a member of the by then defunct *Chit-Yuet* Camphorwood Chests Workers' Guild, although I have no direct proof of this. In any event, the workers left the factory on July 11 but they *'left their tools in the factory* as a sign that they considered themselves to be still employed' (Commissioner of Labor 1951–2:33, emphasis added). A meeting took place between representatives of the workers at George Zee & Co. and the Labor Department on July 17 after the manager of the factory had posted notices threatening the workers with dismissal if they did not return to work. The workers then put forward the additional demand that their foreman, who was thought to have been fired, be reinstated, and made various complaints about sanitary conditions in the factory 'which on investigation were proved to be due to the fact that the cleaning staff were not carrying out their work' (Commissioner of Labor 1951–2:33).

Throughout the strike, the workers denied belonging to any union, and the strike remained confined to one factory. The demands were accepted, but a further demand by the workers that the new piecework rate be made retroactive was refused and the strike continued till July 20. There is no indication if the final demand was accepted in full or not.

Later in the year, another dispute arose at George Zee & Co. over the actions of the manager who, in compliance with factory regulations, had prevented workers from sleeping in the factory. It was during this dispute that the Camphorwood Trunk Workers' Union surfaced as the designated representative of the discontented workers. The Labor Department withdrew from the dispute when the union refused to submit proof of its representation of the striking workers, and the strike was prolonged as a result. The dispute was finally settled within the factory after a compromise was worked out.

A total of 1740 man-days was lost during 1951 at George Zee & Co., according to the Labor Department Report — 540 in the first dispute involving sixty workers from July 11 to July 20, and 1200 in the second dispute from September 1 to September 20. The fact that the second dispute also involved sixty workers would seem to indicate that perhaps it was the same sixty workers in each case. It does not seem unreasonable to suggest that, by the second dispute in their factory, the workers were ready to claim representation by a union to get their point of view across better.

The 1951 disputes at George Zee & Co. are significant for a number of reasons. In the first place, apart from a minor dispute involving the dismissal of a worker and lasting only ten days, which was confined to Yiu On Co., the unrest at George Zee & Co. was the only major disturbance in the industry in the 1950s, and its prolongation seems to have occurred more as a result of the actions of the Hong Kong government than of the proprietor.

The early 1950s in Hong Kong saw an enormous and unprecedented investment of capital in industry, and government became concerned for the first time that conditions for industrial development should remain favorable. In addition to issuing regulations whose effects compromised what had until that time been considered *de facto* privileges of workers, such as the right to sleep and gamble in the factory of one's employ, the government, in the form of the Labor Department, now manifested itself in somewhat greater measure in the arbitration of industrial disputes arising out of enforcement of its law.

It was stepped-up enforcement of government regulations that infringed on workers' traditional privileges in 1951, and it is probable that the workers' wage demands would have been granted and they would have returned to work with less commotion had compliance with government regulations not been at issue.

In Republican times, commentators on Chinese guild practices noted the ease with which workers were able to secure increases in wages. Burgess and Gamble both suggested that this was because employers, having often been workers themselves, or who worked side by side with their workers, were in close touch with workers' needs (Burgess 1928:194; Gamble 1921:184). Wages were adjusted regularly to keep workers at a standard of living deemed customary in a given industry (p. 43). Burgess notes that, prior to 1924, carpenters in Peking had been granted increases six times in six years (Burgess 1928:94). It is conceivable that the relative industrial peace which prevailed in the art-carved furniture industry during the 1950s could be traced to such customary practice.

Gamble also noted that bosses often yielded to workers' demands for the expressed purpose of avoiding government intervention (Gamble 1921:180–1). If a strike 'goes so far as to endanger public tranquility, magistrates interpose, and the strikers being too numerous to be flogged and too poor to pay for the mulcting operation, hands are laid upon the masters, who can always be had when fleecing is feasible; and they to avoid such result of a strike wisely surrender' (Gamble 1921:180–1).

It is likely that, following the dispute at George Zee & Co., the proprietors of art-carved furniture establishments actively avoided the intervention of the government in their relations with workers by avoiding hostile confrontations with their workers in the nine years which were to follow, if for somewhat different reasons. Such factors may account at least in part for the period of industrial peace which prevailed in the art-carved furniture industry through the 1950s.

The first real test of strength between labor and capital occurred in 1960 when workers went out on strike for higher wages (p. 17). This year had marked the climax of economic success and accumulation of capital in the art-carved furniture industry under a regime of 'manufacture', and initiated a period in which strikes occurred with greater regularity, as competing unions came to demand a greater share of the industry's prosperity.

The Report of the Commissioner of Labor for 1960–1 states:

Two unions, the Kong Kong Kowloon Woodwork Carvers' Union and the Hong Kong Kowloon Camphorwood Trunk Workers' Union attempted to negotiate separately for higher wages and better terms of service. These broke down and the first union resorted to strike action for about ten days in May, 1960, resulting in the loss of about 4,950 man-days. The department intervened and agreement was reached on the basis of increases of 20% piece-rates, and $1/day for daily rates. These terms were not acceptable to the Hong Kong Kowloon Camphorwood Trunk Workers' Union and early in June, 1960, the second union also resorted to strike action. After a loss of a further 14,800 man-days, the strike was called off on July 10, 1960. An agreement, effective from May 16, 1960 was signed in the department two days later embodying a 22% increase in piece-rates, reduction in working hours from ten to nine daily, and 12 days' holiday a year with pay. Altogether a total loss of 19,750 man-days, the highest for any particular dispute during the year occurred (Commissioner of Labor 1960–1: 38).

The political divisions of the labor force, which were to disrupt the unity of labor in its dealings with capital for the next ten years, were now manifest. The communist and nationalist unions carried on separate negotiations. Despite the fact that the declared membership in the communist Woodwork Carvers' Union in that year was 516 workers, greater than the combined total of workers in both the nationalist unions, it was the numerically inferior nationalist forces which held out longer for a slightly better settlement. Implicit in the actions of the nationalist group was the desire to prove the superiority of its political stripe by winning greater gains for its constituents. Had labor stood united, it would seem likely that even better terms could have been won for all.

Nevertheless, despite its divisions, organized labor had signalled the end of

74

the era of industrial peace. Not to be caught unawares in the future, the art-carved furniture shop and factory proprietors organized the Hong Kong Kowloon Art-Carved Furniture and Camphorwood Chests Merchants' Association* as the bargaining agent for capital in the same year, 1960. When the next strike occurred in the industry in 1964, they were prepared to take full advantage of all the traditional as well as political divisions within the ranks of their workers. In addition, by 1964, the introduction of power-driven machinery had increased the capital requirements of a competitive production unit of art-carved furniture manufacture, which increasingly alienated the workers from the tools of their trade, and widened considerably the income gulf between worker and boss.

On June 24, 1964, when the Woodwork Carvers' Union presented a demand to the Merchants' Association for an increase of 35% in piecework rates and H.K.$3 a day in daily rates, and six more days' paid holiday a year effective from July 1, the Merchants' Association was prepared. Its leaders replied by stating that before anything could be discussed they must first consult with the other two unions, the Camphorwood Trunk Workers' Union and the Artistic Woodworkers' Union. Furthermore, they stated that any wage agreement reached should take effect as from September 1 (Commissioner of Labor 1964–5:68).

The Woodwork Carvers' Union would not agree to these conditions, and called its constituent carvers, carpenters and painters out on strike. Although its registered membership was only 246 workers, the Merchants' Association estimated that some 600 carvers, 200 painters and 160 carpenters responded to this initial strike call (Commissioner of Labor 1964–5:68).

By the middle of July, the other two unions had made their demands known, the Camphorwood Trunk Workers' Union demanding a 40% increase in piece-rates and a H.K.$3 a day increase in day-wages, while the Artistic Woodworkers asked for a 37% increase in piece-rate and H.K.$2.50 in day-wages.

On July 25, the Merchants' Association held a general meeting and presented an offer of 15% increase in piece-rates and H.K.75¢ in day-wages. This was communicated to the Woodwork Carvers' Union on July 27, with the request that the strike be called off and negotiations continued. The union refused.

During August, the Merchants' Association was able to take advantage of the divisions inherent in the synthetic structure of art-carved furniture production in its 'manufacturing' phase. A group of painters, whose caste-like status has already been mentioned (p. 51) grew restless as the strike moved into its second month and concluded an independent agreement with the Merchants' Association for an increase of 20% in piece-rates, and H.K.$1 a day in day-rates, provided they returned to work. Many did, and according to the Labor Department, many other workers followed, and the back of the strike was effectively broken.

The two nationalist unions continued negotiations with the Merchants' Association 'in a friendly atmosphere' (Commissioner of Labor 1964–5:69)

* See Chapter 7.

and on September 29 formal terms were agreed upon and signed in the Labor Department. Carvers and painters got a 22% increase in piece-rates and H.K.$1.10 increase in day-wages to be effective from August 1, while carpenters got a 27% increase in piece-rates and a H.K.$1.35 increase in day-wages. The higher increases for carpenters were designed to try to win back carpenters who had left the art-carved furniture industry for higher-paying construction jobs. The building boom was in progress in 1964 and carpenters were in short supply.

The Woodwork Carvers' Union never came to a formal agreement with the Merchants' Association in 1964, but later claimed in the local press that it had succeeded in exacting more favorable terms for its members from individual employers (Commissioner of Labor 1964–5:69).

All of the divisions of the labor force which have been touched on were thus manifest in the 1964 dispute, which lasted over three months. While labor came away with moderate gains, it was the Merchants' Association that occupied center-stage in its maneuverings and dealings with separate groups of its divided labor force, and that succeeded in undermining the power of its striking workers.

Another work stoppage occurred in 1967 when communist workers answered the call for a general strike put forward by the communist Hong Kong Federation of Trade Unions. In 1967 there were large-scale riots throughout Hong Kong, triggered initially by a lockout at a plastic flowers factory in Kowloon. Anti-British sentiment ran high, fueled by stepped-up anti-imperialist propaganda radiating from the Mainland, then in the midst of its Great Proletarian Cultural Revolution (see Ta Kung Pao 1967).

The art-carved furniture workers were apparently able to secure an increase in wages during the 1967 strike, although it remains uncertain whether the strike in the art-carved furniture industry, *per se*, was precipitated with this specific goal in mind. Carved-furniture factory proprietors were an unlikely target for anti-imperialist sentiment, and the few workers who did mention the 1967 strike in the industry in their survey responses, characterized it primarily as an expression of sympathy for the wider anti-imperialist activities then being organized throughout Hong Kong. It is, however, likely that the left-wing union took advantage of the widespread unrest in Hong Kong to extract a wage increase from the Merchants' Association at that time.

Following the 1967 disturbances, the *Far Eastern Economic Review* has claimed that the Peking government, dissatisfied with their Hong Kong compatriots' handling of the unrest, called a halt to the fomenting of revolutionary activities in the Crown Colony (see *Far Eastern Economic Review* July 6, 1967:40; July 27, 1967:217; August 10, 1967:307). Just how accurate these claims are is probably debateable. However, it is widely admitted in the Hong Kong pro-communist community that Peking wanted a stable situation in Hong Kong so that it could actively pursue what, from its viewpoint, were more pressing diplomatic questions such as entry into the United Nations and the liberation of Taiwan. In the words of today's pro-communist journalists, 'Hong Kong is a historical problem that will be solved at the appropriate time'. The Hong Kong 'problem' does not have the status of a 'principle' contradiction for the Peoples' Republic. For the moment, Hong Kong remains valuable to the Communist Chinese in terms of the significant amounts of foreign exchange which China earns by marketing its products in and through the port, and also as a place in which trade and diplomatic contacts between China and western countries can be pursued conveniently. Such functions may decline as China continues to open up diplomatically and economically, but they were still important during my stay in 1972–4.

In any case, in the post-1967 period, industrial peace in Hong Kong was the common desire of the British Colonial government and the Communist government in Peking. Unions affiliated with the pro-Peking Hong Kong Federation of Trade Unions were undoubtedly affected. While it is virtually impossible to ascertain just how much control the Federation exercises over its constituent unions, it is probable that when an affiliated union decides to make a wage demand, it must be cleared with the Federation, which means the demand is evaluated not only in terms of the workers' immediate needs, such as coping with a rising cost of living, but also in terms of the effects any increase might have on the political situation *vis-à-vis* the British, and *vis-à-vis* the Peking government and its relations with the British. In the art-carved furniture industry these effects are not likely to be as great as they might be in textiles, plastics or electronics, which are the mainstays of Hong Kong's prosperity, or in public utilities. However, in all, one gets the impression that the Woodwork Carvers' Union has been restricted to some extent since 1967 in its plans for industrial action, in deference to policy commitments and requirements of the Peking government, whose immediate goals do not always coincide neatly with Hong Kong workers' needs.

This contradiction between the interests of the Hong Kong worker in his own material well-being and the requirement that he subordinate his immediate interests to the long-run national interests of Peking, has surely not made life easy for the constituent unions of the pro-communist Hong Kong Federation of Trade Unions in their organizing efforts in the post-1967 Hong Kong setting. Nevertheless, in more recent years, as Peking pursued the resolution of what it took to be principal contradictions, namely admission to the United Nations and the liberation of Taiwan, developments in Hong Kong tended to bear out the appropriateness of their strategy. In 1971 when the Peking government displaced the Taiwan government as the sole legitimate representative of the Chinese people at the United Nations, the political influence that Peking was able to exercise in the political balance of Hong Kong grew enormously at the expense of the Nationalists. Organs of Peking power like the Hong Kong Federation of Trade Unions gained an enormous legitimacy in the new aura that came to surround the Peking government. Allegiance to the Peoples'

Republic, long an obstacle to effective organization among Hong Kong's largely political refugee population, became somewhat more of an asset for groups like the Woodwork Carvers' Union. 1971 marked a turning point in the fortunes of their organizing. Indeed one could argue that the relegation of the Hong Kong 'problem' to the status of a secondary contradiction made a great deal of sense as the political balance in Hong Kong tipped noticeably in favor of the Peking government in the course of the resolution of a higher order contradiction manifest in its seating at the United Nations.

All this should not be construed as implying that the Woodwork Carvers' Union was totally paralyzed between 1967 and 1971, or that it gained nothing from its affiliation with the communist Federation of Trade Unions. It was a willing partner and continues to be so. Two strikes have occurred in the industry since 1967 and it is clear that the Federation came to the union's aid with strike pay, food, meeting space and resources the likes of which a minor union like the Woodwork Carvers' Union could probably never muster on its own.

In addition, the Federation encourages a unity and cameraderie with workers in other affiliated unions that promotes class consciousness among the workers and also keeps them informed of events on the Mainland. Copies of *China Pictorial* and *China Reconstructs* are provided to members each month. Membership in an affiliated union may also facilitate return trips to one's native village in China during New Year and at other times as well, since the Federation provides a link up with Chinese representatives and bureaucracy in Hong Kong. Thus while it is my general impression that the Woodwork Carvers' Union has been acting with restraint in presenting its wage demands since 1967, they have been vigorously supported by the Federation in securing those minimum demands for their workers.

The late 1960s witnessed an increasing concentration of capital in units of art-carved furniture production and, as has been mentioned, a progressive alienation of workers from the tools of their trade. Bosses began to withdraw with greater frequency from the work process, behind permanent office staffs and administrative subordinates. If one were to argue that relations between boss and workers were still close and informal in factories like Heng Lung Co. in 1973, and that this closeness was still a factor in the boss's willingness to grant wage increases to his workers, it would nevertheless still have to be admitted that the strength of this closeness and informality will probably decline sharply over the next few years. Under these circumstances, a strong union, which is able to take advantage of local labor scarcity, and good communications with an effective organizational strategy will be increasingly important in protecting the interests of labor.

The Woodwork Carvers' Union

The Woodwork Carvers' Union already seems well geared to this task. Its premises are a center of continuous activity designed to instill class identity in its workers. It is a dormitory for some, recreation center for others. The union provides its members with many benefits through its access to organs of Communist Chinese power in Hong Kong and it has gone through an effective membership drive which both expanded and consolidated its representation of workers in the art-carved furniture industry. It has taken many of the institutions and practices which characterized traditional guild organization and instilled them with new content, making them serve new purposes more consistent with the changing state of the productive forces and relations of production in the industry. The international diplomatic turn in favor of the Peking government has greatly increased its power *vis-à-vis* its Nationalist adversaries and, in 1973, it stood poised on the point of becoming the sole representative of workers in the art-carved furniture industry.

The activities of the Woodwork Carvers' Union which I witnessed during my apprenticeship and investigation of the art-carved furniture trade in 1972–3 clearly indicate its vitality.

In mid-April, 1973, I began to hear about an impending demand for a raise in pay and, early in May, I was invited to attend the yearly mass-meeting of the Woodwork Carvers' Union, at which the demand was to be formally announced. It took place on the evening of May 18. My fieldnotes of that day are reproduced below, interspersed with biographical sketches of some of the officers, also extracted from my fieldnotes:

Friday night, I attended the 21st anniversary meeting of the founding of the Woodwork Carvers' Union. It was held in a large auditorium in Tokwawan in a building which houses many offices and organizations of the Hong Kong 'patriotic' (pro-communist Chinese) movement. When the program started, the room was just full with perhaps 700–800 people, and a larger number of women and children than I had expected to see. It was really a family affair as the later entertainment was to prove. Contrary to my expectations, there was no food provided except for a small bag of sweets given each guest, and I grew increasingly hungry as the evening wore on.

The program began with an address by the Chairman of the Union, a Zhejiang native (from Dongyang) who has been Chairman for many years, although I was never able to find out just how many.

(The Chairman is generally not very talkative. He seldom chairs meetings that occur at union headquarters and this is probably due to his thick Zhejiang accent which is often difficult for the Cantonese speakers who occupy the majority of other union posts, and who comprise the majority of other members to understand. It may also account for his apparent shyness and usual infrequency of speech. He does not fit the bill as a labor racketeer, although a fair degree of political savvy must have been necessary for him to have maintained his position as Chairman for as long as he has. It is conceivable that his position as Chairman is partly honorary, but what the honor is, or in recognition of what traits the honor was bestowed, is not readily obvious. He does seem quite

capable and intelligent, and perhaps in the past ten or so years that he is supposed to have been Chairman of the union, he took on more responsibility for
the day to day running of the union than at present. While the number of
Cantonese speaking workers in the industry has grown at a higher rate than
Zhejiang/Shanghainese speakers in the post-war period, and while this may
have diminished the Chairman's effectiveness as a leader, there are still large
numbers of bosses of Zhejiang/Shanghai origins in the industry, and it may be
convenient to maintain a Zhejiang native union Chairman to carry out negotiations.)

The Chairman addressed the assembly standing before a portrait of Chairman
Mao Tse-tung, and his speech stressed the accomplishments of the Chinese nation
in the recent past. He also touched on the skyrocketing cost of living in Hong
Kong at present [1973], a theme dwelt upon again and again during the evening.

Next on the program occurred the swearing in of new officers, who were
called out on stage, turned to face the portrait of Chairman Mao and the Chinese
flag and recited Mao Tse-tung's 'Serve the People' in unison. There are twelve
officers and another seven members of the executive committee. The officers
are Chairman, Vice-Chairman, Secretary, Treasurer, Organization Secretary,
Investigations Officer, Welfare Officer, Propaganda Officer, Communications
Officer, Entertainment Officer and several others.

Both the Chairman and Vice-Chairman have apparently served more than
ten years, and the yearly election which precedes the annual meeting seems to
return the same officers year after year, with a few jugglings among the less
important officers. As I was unable to obtain officer lists for any year except the
present [1973], it is only my impression that the lesser offices are held with
less regularity than those of higher rank, and it is altogether possible that the
same people are also returned to the lower ranking offices year in, year out
[see Burgess 1928:136 and Gamble 1921:178 on rotation of guild offices].

The crowd was then addressed by an official of the Federation of Trade
Unions. An elderly man, his voice didn't carry and his words were barely intel-
ligible. Background noise from the huge fans, as well as the constant hum of
conversation of friends in the audience didn't help much.

The most important speaker of the evening was the organization secretary,
whose speech was clear and concise and who held the audience with his speaking
power. He stated that prices, rents, etc., were so high that an increase in wages
was now necessary. Their demand was to be a H.K.$5/day increase in daily
wages and a 25% increase in piece wages. Apparently contacts had been made
with the Nationalist Camphorwood Trunk Workers' Union to inform them of
the wage demands so that if they too were going to push wage demands this year,
the right hand would know what the left hand was doing, so to speak. The
organization secretary reported that more than 10 bosses had already agreed to
the raise to take effect on June 1. He stated that if all else failed there would be
a strike and urged all the workers to stand united and strongly support their
just demands. Nevertheless he also cautioned against the likelihood of, or
necessity for strike action. He was a fiery speaker, by far the most effective of
the evening and seemed not to be reading from a prepared text.

(The organization secretary is probably one of the most intelligent of the current union officers. Very bright, gregarious, lucid and expressive, he under-stood my desire for information better and more clearly than most other union members, realizing that much of the information I had gathered from the workers in the industry might be of value to the union. My refusal to divulge information obtained in confidence during extensive interviews disappointed him although he understood my ethical reasons for refusing. At weekly union meetings, he always had something to contribute to the ongoing work or business at hand, in the form of ideas or actions, which almost always made sense. He took his union duties very seriously).

The organization secretary's speech was followed on the program rather anti-climactically by the poor Vice-Chairman, who had a difficult time following the preceding act. There was not very much he could add.

(Much of the day to day work of the union is overseen by the Vice-Chairman. Also a quiet type, he exudes a kind of confidence in his own abilities that instills trust in him by all members. He normally sets the tone at meetings, never loses his composure, and other workers usually wait for him to speak first when some-thing is to be discussed or when the proper conclusions must be drawn. He takes his time and then speaks, always summing up carefully and concisely, pointing out the appropriate lessons to be learned. A family man, he occasionally brings his three-year-old child up to the headquarters and shows himself both kind and firm, so that his kid always seems well-behaved and at peace with his father. Were the Vice-Chairman not occupying the position he does, I believe the union would be hard pressed to find anyone as capable to fill his shoes.)

Following the Vice-Chairman's speech, the business part of the meeting ended, and the entertainment began, performances being given by a 'patriotic' troop hired for the occasion. One number was performed by the children of the school at the Woodwork Carvers' Union premises. The evening was capped by a pro-union play of the *Waiting for Lefty* agit-prop type, in which a worker injured on the job learns how really insecure his position as a proletarian is with nothing but his own labor to sell. Unless he stands united with his fellow workers in a union, he really has no chance of supporting his family with his now injured arm, as his boss refuses to take him back on the job. He is attended to by a union doctor and two union members, having no money to see a private doctor. Gradually he and his wife come to see the benefits of union membership and the play ends happily with all setting out to attend the union meeting.

There were also dances to revolutionary themes with dancers dressed in costumes of Chinese people in various walks of life and one dance depicting the victories won by the Chinese Peoples' Liberation Army. The troop had its own Chinese-style orchestra which rendered the tunes to accompany the dances.

A broadsheet was published for the occasion in which a yearly union budget for 1972–3 was printed, showing a total of H.K.$15,917.55 income and H.K.$9,544.79 expenditure. The greater share of income was accounted for by monthly dues totalling H.K.$14,068 while close to H.K.$1,000 was earned in bank interest. Of expenditure, the largest amount spent was under the category of *xin jin tie*, a rather ambiguous term which takes in subsidies, allowances, gratuities, assistance, and which might also include bribes, or even scholarships, or a form of workman's compensation. A total of H.K.$4,290 was spent in this category. The second largest category of expense was for the yearly anniversary meeting and celebration costing H.K.$1,124.95.

Operating under a separate budget was the social welfare section, which spent H.K.$3,766, and took in H.K.$3,815. Of expenses for welfare, a total of H.K. $1,286 was spent on payments to sick or injured workers, and H.K.$1,800 in general welfare expenses.

Selection of officers, announcement of wage demands, and reports of expenditure were noted by Burgess among the items of business normally conducted at the annual meetings of traditional Chinese guilds (Burgess 1928:145). While a religious service honoring the guild founder was usually part of the program, both Burgess and Morse had already noted the decline or absence of religious ceremonies or common guild worship in the early twentieth century (Burgess 1928:176 and Morse 1909:17). The absence of such services at the yearly meeting of the Woodwork Carvers' Union is not of any singular importance.

However, other portions of the traditional program of annual guild meetings have been preserved, although in somewhat revised form. Gamble noted that musical performances, operas and plays were a typical occurrence at yearly guild meetings (Gamble 1921:171), and the Woodwork Carvers' Union preserves the form of these presentations, substituting an updated political content more consistent with its pro-communist ideology, and with the increasingly proletarianized character of work relations in the industry.

The wage demands presented at the meeting in 1973 were granted in full by the Merchants' Association. On May 31 an article appeared in *Wen Wei Bao*, a news organ of communist persuasion, congratulating the workers on the acceptance of their demands by the Merchants' Association. Although I have no idea what occurred during the negotiations, I do know that the raise was granted in full, the only concession that the Merchants' Association was able to extract being a delay in the date from which the raise was to take effect from June 1 to June 15. Early in June, when I went to the union headquarters, a copy of the agreement was hung on the union bulletin board, signed and chopped by officers of both union and Association, and the wage increase was thus officially assured. No strike was necessary.

The current premises of the union are in an apartment block in Tokwawan in Kowloon. They occupy a flat decorated with Communist slogans and a picture of Chairman Mao Tse-tung flanked by two Chinese flags. The federation of Trade Unions runs a small school for children of 'patriotic' workers in the union headquarters, but the children are not necessarily those of art-carved furniture workers. The union premises are seldom used by the workers before evening, as they are all working, and the flat was made available to the Federation for the operation of the school. The flat therefore contains rows of moveable student desks and stools, and one wall is covered by a blackboard used during the day at the school. Shortly before I left Hong Kong, this school was discontinued and the teacher, a middle-school graduate, went to work in a factory. I do not know why the school was discontinued, except that it never catered to more than ten children at one time and perhaps was considered uneconomic.

Other Federation-affiliated unions have also used the flat for meetings and other activities, such as preparing for the celebrations of October 1, the anniversary of the founding of the Peoples' Republic of China. The premises are, however, under the control of the Woodwork Carvers' Union, and it is my impression that any such use of their premises by Federation-affiliated unions must be approved by them.

In September 1973, the flat received a fresh coat of paint, and the faded slogans were taken down for repainting, in preparation for the October 1 celebration. Member-painters donated labor so the cost was minimal if not nil. The celebration itself was held in a restaurant large enough to accommodate the several hundred members who would attend. I was unfortunately not invited and so I cannot report in detail on the proceedings.

The flat serves as a place where workers without the means to afford a private apartment in Hong Kong's over-inflated real estate market, and without family in Hong Kong to take care of them, may sleep at night. However, one must be prepared to put up with the regulations, which include lights out and lock up at 11.00 p.m. One worker-friend of mine, forced by circumstances to stay temporarily at the union, had a serious disagreement with the union because of these regulations. Nevertheless, during the year that I was acquainted with the union, two or three workers made the union premises their more or less permanent dwelling place. There were no bunk beds in the Woodwork Carvers' Union premises, although I observed them built into the walls of other union halls I visited in Hong Kong. Workers just unrolled their bedrolls across boards which had been laid across the students' desks.

Once every week or two, these same desks were pulled together to form a long table, and the officers and 'activists' in the union would hold a meeting. Attendance was usually upwards of twenty people and various items of union business were dealt with. These included such things as a response to a letter from the Registry of Trade Unions of the Hong Kong Government; preparations for the October 1 celebration; discussion of the wage raise to be demanded and ultimately attained in 1973; planning of a picnic which was to take place on the birthday of the historic founder of the carpentry and carving trades, *Luban* (discussed below pp. 87–8), etc.

On occasion, a representative from the Federation of Trade Unions would sit in on a meeting to see how the union was faring, bringing with him or her news of significance to the labor movement in general for workers to discuss. These discussions were usually fairly lively, most participants doing their best to give a favorable impression of the workings of their union.

The wood-carvers of Hong Kong

Once a month, the union receives copies of a Federation of Trade Unions newspaper entitled *Hong Kong Worker* in which various sorts of articles concerning the situation of the working class in Hong Kong appear. There are also articles about China, explanations of current policy initiatives, sports news, a regular women's column and political cartoons as well. On March 29, 1973, I was invited to sit in on a discussion of the articles in the latest issue. The headline article concerned the recent death of several construction workers who had fallen from scaffolding during the construction of the new Connaught Center Building on Hong Kong Island. A free-ranging discussion followed the reading aloud of the article, with those workers who could read with facility taking turns reading successive paragraphs. Industrial safety and industrial accidents in Hong Kong were the main topic of the discussion and the question of how this topic applied to workers in the art-carved furniture industry was raised and discussed as well. Lest one think the extrapolation to the furniture industry a bit strained, Labor Department figures for industrial accidents for the first four months of 1973 'were the worst in Hong Kong's history, with an average of one death and 70 injuries every day' (*Hong Kong Standard*, June 29, 1973).

A surprisingly high degree of class identity was expressed by the workers during the discussion, and the question of industrial safety was linked to relations between workers and capitalists, the drive for profit, lack of concern for workers' welfare, etc. The sessions occur on a regular basis coinciding with the monthly publication of *Hong Kong Worker* and were known as 'discussions of our livelihood'. I was also present at the union headquarters on several other occasions when such discussions were in progress, usually chaired by the Vice-Chairman, and involving anywhere from ten to twenty workers.

On June 29, 1973, a similar discussion occurred, this one concerning developments in Shanxi province, printed and sent round in a circular by the Federation of Trade Unions. The article was also read aloud paragraph by paragraph, but the discussion was not as lengthy as that which accompanied the reading of *Hong Kong Worker*. The event seemed designed to promote national consciousness as opposed to class consciousness, and the news did not seem to affect the lives of the art-carved furniture workers as directly as did the articles in *Hong Kong Worker*. Nevertheless, the policy of the Peoples' Republic of China with respect to Hong Kong residents includes encouraging individual Chinese to declare the Peoples' Republic as the object of their national loyalty, of their 'patriotism', and a steady stream of news concerning the accomplishments of the Peoples' Republic is filtered down through the Federation, with the aim of instilling in the workers a pride in their homeland, occasionally at the expense of their own class interests.

This nationalist component of Chinese Communist policy toward Hong Kong is also manifest in the preferential treatment accorded China's 'national' as opposed to 'compradore' bourgeoisie in Hong Kong. The pro-Peking 'patriotic' community in Hong Kong includes some rather wealthy businessmen who deal in Chinese commodities either exclusively, or in part, or who rely on Communist China for raw materials or equipment for their businesses. This can sometimes lead to the bizarre configuration of a pro-Peking employers' association negotiating with a pro-Taipei union of workers over wage demands, as was the case in the ivory-carving industry.

Union representatives come in from time to time with dues they have collected in their particular geographical area, laying the money and receipts before the treasurer, who enters the transactions carefully into the books. The representative may also pick up the latest copy of *China Pictorial* or *China Reconstructs* to distribute to the union members in his area. He keeps a careful checklist of who has received one every month. Sometimes a union representative will bring an application form from a worker who has just joined the union, together with three pictures, one of which is pasted in a huge membership book along with a great deal of personal data — name, place of origin, age, date of birth, date of first registration, address, etc. — another is affixed to a small certificate of membership, and a third goes into a small, red, numbered membership book, which the worker keeps in his possession at all times, and which has a space for stamping receipt of dues, as well as a list of union regulations. A numbered badge is also given out to new members, on which is embossed a yellow star on a red background, with the carpenter's hammer, the carver's carving tool, and the painter's brush crossed beneath and tied with a ribbon, and the union's name around the lower perimeter (see Figure 3).

Figure 3. Union badge

The union keeps scrupulous records of every action and transaction that occurs within its purview. Every member who has given money, bought a ticket, received a magazine, or whatever, is given a receipt for his every transaction, all of which are dutifully recorded in the account books.

In August–September 1973, a membership drive began and a chart posted on the bulletin board showed, in bar graphs, the increases in membership for the various districts in which art-carved furniture factories are located: Cheung Sha

The wood-carvers of Hong Kong

Wan, San Po Kong, K'un T'ong, Chun Shek Shan (Diamond Hill), Tsimshatsui and New Territories/Tsuen Wan. K'un T'ong was well in the lead. This is the site of the largest carving factories in Hong Kong, where it could be argued the concentration of capital, and the alienation of the worker from his tools and from his product have progressed furthest. According to the union vice-chairman, about 200 additional members were recruited in 1973, bringing membership at that time up to somewhere around 700 workers.

On one occasion I saw the actual recruitment of a new member in progress at Heng Lung Co., where I worked. There was quite an enthusiastic union member working there, one who had been back to visit his native village in Guangdong province in the Xin Hui district several times, coming back with glowing reports about the progress of his home village under socialism. He even had arguments with other workers in the factory about the accuracy of his observations and reports. This man began to proselytize a younger worker in the factory, about 28 years old. The younger worker had previously explained to me that he had no interest in the union or anything political at all. But as they worked the enthusiastic cadre began talking to him about the union, and invited him to a weekly meeting. The younger worker gave no indication whether he would go or even whether he was willing to go. Finally, he went, was introduced to all the members and officers there by his fellow worker, and joined the union. While I have no idea what his thoughts on the matter actually were, the episode shows clearly how the membership drive in progress was implemented at the factory level.

On any given weekday evening at union headquarters, there may be three or four Chinese chess games in progress with a number of spectators standing around giving advice on which pieces to move. Anyone near enough to give advice to one or another of the players usually does, and any given game serves as a focus for endless voicing and countervoicing of opinion as to what constitutes the right move. There is also a chance that when one enters the union premises there may be a game of bumper checker pool in progress, involving four participants and a great ruckus about the board. One may be teased to within an inch of one's life for a poorly executed shot.

Mah-jong is significantly absent as a diversion at union premises, although it is played regularly at union halls not affiliated with the pro-communist Federation of Trade Unions. It would not, however, be true to say that many pro-communist union members of the art-carved furniture industry never play the game.

On the lunar calendar date of the birthday of the patron saint of workers in wood and construction, Luban (Plate 5), the industry closes down and signs are posted on factory doors explaining the reason (see Chapter 7 for more information on Luban). The Woodwork Carvers' Union, being of communist persuasion, does not engage much in such 'feudal' customs as temple worship or offerings to their craft's founder, although such ceremonies are still carried out

5. The image of master Luban (Luban Temple, Kennedy Town, Hong Kong)

at Luban's temple in Kennedy Town, which is maintained in part from contributions from unions in other construction trades, and in small measure by the Merchants' Association in the art-carved furniture industry.

Most of the members of the Woodwork Carvers' Union, however, take the occasion of their founder's birthday to enjoy themselves in more secular fashion. I was invited to join a union picnic in mid-July, 1973, only to discover in the course of the day, that it was also Luban's birthday according to the lunar calendar:

Today, went on the union picnic and a really fine trip it was. The union hired a boat to Ch'eung Chau (one of the outlying islands, which together with Hong Kong island, Kowloon and the New Territories make up the Crown Colony of Hong Kong) and we spent the day swimming, hiking and playing basketball

87

till I nearly fell dead from exhaustion. Many tables of mah-jong in evidence. The usual crowd from the union hall was there and a remarkable number of faces I had never seen before. Wives and kids were in abundance and a really nice day was had by all. As it turns out, today was *Luban's* birthday and the entire industry had the day off. The boatride back was spent with games for the kids; anagrams of Chinese characters to be arranged into pro-communist Chinese slogans; guessing the number of plums in a bag; answering riddles that implied the names of Chinese leaders, cities, etc. Small prizes were given out to the winners, who very often were those most able to get their fathers' help. The games were enjoyed by all (my fieldnotes, July 12, 1973).

The picnic is interesting in that it again highlights how gracefully the Woodwork Carvers' Union steps into the traditional structure of craft production, revising its significance. The union makes the tradition its own by observing the holiday of the birthday of its traditional founder, but it does so very much on its own terms, and the observation is governed in practice by an ideology consistent with support of the Peoples' Republic of China. There are no religious ceremonies or offerings.

There are still remnants of traditional craft and guild social structure in evidence in the structure and practice of the pro-communist Woodwork Carvers' Union, as well as in the divisions of the labor force which it represents. However, their significance has declined as a result of a combination of economic (e.g. increasing concentration of capital), political (e.g. international recognition of Communist China) and social (e.g. decreasing significance of place of origin) factors which have shaped the development of the mode of production of art-carved furniture on the one hand, and, on the other, as a result of the conscious adaptation and incorporation of traditional practices into the organizational repertoire of the Woodwork Carvers' Union, making these older customs serve new purposes.

The Woodwork Carvers' Union has always encouraged the growth of a modern, unified, class-conscious labor force. These ideas were somewhat in advance of the level of the productive forces and relations of production of art-carved furniture of the 1950s and early 1960s, in which traditional craft parochialism was still the dominant characteristic of the material and ideological conditions of production. The union's ability to weather the struggles of the 1960s, and its current vitality in active promotion of its members' interests in welfare, recreation and livelihood, are expressions of the fact that a more thoroughly proletarianized labor force than that which characterized the regime of 'manufacture' has, for the past ten years, been in process of coming into being. The purposes which the Woodwork Carvers' Union has made its own now command a greater importance in the lives of most workers than ever before. A conjunction of economic, political and social forces have made it possible for the Woodwork Carvers' Union to emerge in the 1970s as the dominant voice in expressing the interests and will of the workers in the art-carved furniture industry.

Politics, and proletarian politics at that, is in command, and the traditional array of discrete unions for carvers and carpenters of differing native places, in differing woods, is in retreat.

6

Commercial relations, structure and practice

Before discussing in detail the commercial relations and business practices of the art-carved furniture industry, it will be useful to review some of the distinctive economic features of post-war Hong Kong, both to establish a broader setting, and to understand how and where the evolving art-carved furniture industry and its own distinctive commercial structure articulate with the larger capitalist social formation which is Hong Kong.

Prior to World War II, Hong Kong functioned as a trade *entrepôt* linking China to the world capitalist system, having replaced the imperially designated port of trade at Canton as a 'free' trade outpost under British jurisdiction after the Opium War (1842). For 100 years, until the Japanese occupation of the colony in 1941, its commercial sector developed, and merchant houses which came into existence during this period were later to provide indispensable links with export markets for Hong Kong's post-war incipient industrial sector (Phelps-Brown 1971:13). The expertise and institutions of a banking system which was to play an important role in Hong Kong's conversion to an economy dominated by industrial export, also came into existence in this early period.

While both the commercial and banking structures were important in the success of Hong Kong's post-war industrialization, the real impetus came in the form of, firstly, the entrepreneurial skills and capital of an already functioning industrial capitalist class from Shanghai and, secondly, a refugee laboring population which came from many parts of China after 1949 (Wong 1958:5; Owen 1971:149; Phelps-Brown 1971:13). One commentator has characterized Hong Kong's post-war industrial growth as merely a transfer of economic activity from Shanghai to Hong Kong (Owen 1971:149).

Prior to the communist victory in the Chinese civil war in 1949, the uncertainty of the Chinese political situation and the deterioration of the Gold Yuan currency led clever businessmen to buy foreign currency with their Gold Yuan and quickly convert it into machinery and raw materials as a means of preserving value:

Purchases of goods by Chinese merchants from abroad after the war [World War II] ran into huge sums, and when the situation in China seemed to be

90

deteriorating, these merchants gave instructions for shipments to be off-loaded in Hong Kong . . . In 1949, the godowns of Hong Kong held large stocks of machinery for textile mills and other factories, and enormous quantities of cotton and other raw materials consigned to China but which had remained in the Colony. These capital goods were valued at hundreds of millions of dollars and led in time to the setting up of factories in this Colony. Experienced members of financial circles are of the opinion that the flow of capital into Hong Kong suddenly jumped to at least $1,000,000,000,000 in one year [1949–50] (Wong 1958:5).

The art-carved furniture industry was not a capital-intensive one at this time. Its combined total of capital industrywide represented only a minute percentage of that enormous figure. Nevertheless, the industry was begun in earnest in Hong Kong after 1949 by refugees who had been exporting furniture from Shanghai and Canton for fifty to sixty years, with the larger units of capital and probably the greater overall percentage of capital resting in immigrant Shanghai (Zhejiang) hands (particularly in the immediate post-1949 period).

Hong Kong's post-war economic growth record has been quite impressive by Asian standards. In most indices of economic performance it ranks just behind Japan and has only recently taken third place to Singapore. Furthermore, its growth has been stable. 'Only once between 1960 and 1968 did the annual rate of expansion of exports fall below 13% (in 1961) and only once (in 1968) was it above 17%' (England 1971:211). This in itself would have been quite an accomplishment, but at the same time the economy was able to maintain full employment, while absorbing large numbers of refugees every year. In addition, average real wages in industry doubled in the decade 1958–68 and all this was achieved without foreign aid (Phelps-Brown 1971:13).

These are statistics of which any developing nation would be proud, yet, in certain respects, the conditions under which Hong Kong achieved them are not common to social formations of the world capitalist periphery.

The absence of a primary producing sector is one very important reason why Hong Kong's 'model of success' is not really exportable. The bulk of its food supplies are imported from China at prices which increase the tendency of Hong Kong farmers to give up farming marginal lands and move to the city to seek more remunerative industrial employment. This in turn 'generates export earnings worth considerably more in terms of imported food than [the farmer's] agricultural yield on marginal areas' (Owen 1971:153). Furthermore, these cheap food imports from China have contributed to the relative absence of inflation in Hong Kong and have reduced pressure on industrialists to pay higher wages. In effect, 'the communes are subsidizing the capitalists' (England 1971:217).

One commentator has summed up the reasons why Hong Kong does not face the problems of self-supporting subsistence economies which characterize most Third World countries:

The wood-carvers of Hong Kong

Hong Kong both as a free port and a small economy is fortunate in that it can make use of any saleable surpluses of foodstuffs or industrial materials which appear on the world market. The 'wages fund' (total consumption) is, in practice, what it pays the business community to import (i.e. the marginal propensity to import is high); it does not depend upon the capacity of the indigenous population to save, nor upon the efficiency of their food producers. And the work places upon which their capacity to sell their labor to advantage in the world economy depends, are mainly the fruit of surpluses which have emerged elsewhere in the world. Consequently, the really basic problem of economic growth as it appears in mainly self-supporting subsistence economies does not arise in its simplest form (Smith 1966:29).

One unfortunate consequence, however, of this reliance on the world market for its wages fund, raw materials and markets, is the threat of fluctuations in production and employment brought about by variations in demand for finished products, and/or in supply on the world market of raw materials for industry and foodstuffs to feed workers. World food shortages and rising prices have caused the Peoples' Republic of China to increase the price of food sold to Hong Kong so as to stay more in line with international market prices. While these prices remain well below those on the international market, fears of the inflationary effects of increasing food prices were current in the mid-1970s. The proprietors of art-carved furniture establishments in Hong Kong, whose supplies of wood come mostly from southeast Asia — teak from Thailand, Burma and Indonesia, rosewood from Thailand, and camphorwood from Taiwan — have been forced to pay increasing prices for these commodities, and prices for completed merchandise have consequently been rising.

For most industries, international competition places a ceiling on increasing production costs, beyond which the entrepreneur is not free to pass on such increases to the consumer (England 1971:212). As the home market for Hong Kong's manufactures is quite small, protective tariffs cannot shield the entrepreneur from this competition. Tariffs would only provoke retaliation on the part of Hong Kong's trading partners on whose markets Hong Kong is totally dependent. Throughout the 1950s and 1960s Hong Kong's only competitor in the art-carved furniture industry was the Peoples' Republic of China, whose goods were excluded from the largest market for carved-wood products, the United States. This meant that Hong Kong producers of art-carved furniture were relatively free of the constraints of international competition, although competition between Hong Kong producers was, nevertheless, great.

At present, with the United States opening its doors to goods of Communist Chinese manufacture, there has very definitely been a limit placed on the degree to which production costs in Hong Kong's art-carved furniture industry may rise. In 1973, Hong Kong art-carved furniture shared a two-tiered market with art-carved furniture of Mainland Chinese manufacture. The Mainland Chinese product was markedly superior and sold for a higher price.

Commercial relations, structure and practice

Two-tiered markets of this kind were common in Republican Chinese treaty ports (Hou 1965:153). The carpet industry of Tianjin, for example, produced and marketed two different lines of rugs. Those of lesser quality were all but driven out of the market by the development of machine-made, low-quality carpets in the United States in the 1920s, and the imposition of a tariff on low-quality carpets entering the country. The higher grade of carpet was not so excluded, and firms capable of producing the higher grade were unaffected.

At present there are no firms in Hong Kong which could match the higher quality of the Mainland Chinese carved-furniture product, and increasing production and labor costs in Hong Kong are not matched in China where the costs of most production factors are rigorously controlled. Fortunately for the Hong Kong businessman, China's enormous demand for foreign exchange to finance its own economic development has led the Peoples' Republic to increase the prices of its luxury export manufactures. This gives the Hong Kong manufacturer, saddled with rising costs, some room to maneuver, although there are indications that the effects of a recession which occurred in the Hong Kong industry during 1974–5, just after my departure, may have been exacerbated by competition from higher quality Mainland products.

The constraints of this two-tiered market have become an additional factor conducing to diversification into modern styles of furniture, a strategy already adopted by many of Hong Kong's furniture establishments in the 1960s. The market for modern-style furniture is larger and more stable than that for carved curio pieces.

The Hong Kong economy is unusual among developing nations of the world capitalist periphery in its reliance on the export of manufactures. In this it differs fundamentally from most developing countries 'which tend to develop their industries initially to provide substitutes for manufactured articles previously imported from developed countries' (Owen 1971:145). Hong Kong's bourgeoisie adopted a strategy involving specialization in only one of several stages in the planning, design, production and marketing of its products.

Hong Kong offered itself as a workshop producing to the specifications of European, American and later Japanese companies. In this way, many of its firms allied themselves to and complemented rather than competed with the capital and skills of more advanced countries (Owen 1971:154). Amin has argued that this is the only strategy that makes any sense for the national bourgeoisie of the world capitalist periphery (Amin 1974a: 162, 176), and while, as a result, Hong Kong's economy shares the disarticulation of sectors and unevenness of productivity between its sectors that, according to Amin, characterize social formations of the capitalist periphery, Hong Kong has made a virtue of these characteristics.

As there was no question of producing to stimulate growth in a large subsistence sector, the strategy was satisfactory. No questions of balanced growth or control over the profits of industry, as arise in other developing countries, arose in Hong Kong. The market governed direction and reinvestment in industry, and led to the emergence in Hong Kong of a small number of industries with an impressive record of international success (Owen 1971:176). The question of control over and national sovereignty of the fruits of labor was at least temporarily set aside by mutual agreement of the British and Communist Chinese governments to some indefinite time in the future (see below p. 95). The fruits were left for the meantime very much in the hands of the bourgeoisie, both native and international.

Hong Kong's reliance on exports of manufactures had inbuilt advantages:

Export of manufactures offers far more promising growth prospects than primary products — the major export item of South Asian countries. Demand for manufactures tends to rise at least as fast as incomes in developed countries, whereas the demand for primary products tends to lag behind, particularly when they meet competition from synthetic substitutes. Earnings from the export of manufactures are also more stable. Moreover manufactures provide the opportunity of . . . moving up into the better quality end of the product range through experience, better design and improved quality control. Primary products offer little or no opportunity for this (Owen 1971:153).

The opportunity of moving up in the better-quality end of a product range was probably meant to refer to the larger textile and electronics industries. However, the art-carved furniture industry provides an interesting example of how experience in traditional craft production, such as carved-wood furniture, was turned easily to more modern furniture styles where growth prospects in the 1960s were more promising. The increasing demand for carved rosewood products by Japanese buyers in the late 1960s and early 1970s was similarly easily accommodated by many furniture producers who had previously specialized in teak.

The Hong Kong government has created a climate conducive to investment by both its native and international bourgeoisies. In certain respects the government's policy has been reminiscent of the Taoist maxim, *wu wei er wei ye* (by not doing, it is done). 'Market forces are allowed to shape the economy — selecting the industries to be developed and sizes of firms composing them' (Owen 1971:155). 'The government often shows a better understanding of the optimal properties of a market economy than the industrialists who are making a living out of it' and government has resisted the efforts of those who have wanted it to intervene on behalf of certain industrial sectors whose interests were threatened by rigorous international competition (Owen 1971:155–6). Taxes have remained low and stable, legal incorporation easy, and few regulations exist to hamper the entrepreneur in the conduct of his business.

In other respects, for example in the provision of subsidized housing to over 40% of its citizens, the government does actively intervene in the economy. Here it aids the entrepreneur as well as the ordinary citizen, by relieving pressures which might tend to drive rents and thus wage demands up. Owen finds such intervention 'perfectly explicable within the overall *laissez-faire* philosophy' of the Hong Kong government since the market for housing is entirely local, shielded from international competition by factors of location, and is one for which the government possesses reliable indices of demand. It can therefore use funds in support of the housing industry with little risk (Owen 1971:156).

One factor governing the conduct of business in Hong Kong which has been of overriding importance is that of time. For many years the ninety-nine-year lease on the New Territories which is due to expire in 1997 was assumed to represent a deadline after which no one could be certain about the security of his privately invested capital. Most people agree that Hong Kong could not continue to survive independent of the New Territories. The Communist Chinese, however, have recently clarified their position on the lease. Since the treaty ceding Hong Kong to the British and the protocol leasing the New Territories to the British for ninety-nine years were both illegal, their terms are not binding, and presumably China could demand the return of the Crown Colony of Hong Kong at any time at a moment's notice. Ironically, however, this non-recognition of Hong Kong's colonial status has come to serve as a pretext for planning a future for Hong Kong which assumes the extension of the present political *status quo* well beyond the 1997 expiry date of the lease on the New Territories. In 1978, it was fairly certain the Peoples' Republic would continue to tolerate the existence of the 'colony' into the indefinite future.

Until very recently, however, long-range business investment was considered risky, and most businessmen planned to have received back the full value of their invested capital in five years (England 1971:216—17). Businesses tended to seek fast profits, with high rates of capital turnover, and the art-carved furniture industry was no exception. This lent an air of urgency to the business climate within the overall *laissez-faire* economy. The end seemed well in sight.

To pursue the discussion of the commercial relations and business practices of the art-carved furniture industry in this context, Heng Lung Co. serves as a convenient vantage point.

Heng Lung Co.

財源茂盛達三江　　The sources of wealth are bountiful
　　　　　　　　　　　reaching three rivers, in extent.

生意興隆通四海　　Business is prosperous throughout
　　　　　　　　　　　the four seas.*

Heng Lung Co. is located in Ho Ka Yuen, the Ho family garden (Plate 6), a tract of 4.2 acres of land nestled just at the base of the Kowloon foot-hills, northwest of the walled city of Kowloon, and almost due west of the Hau Wong temple

* The saying from which Heng Lung Co. takes its name; hangs in the living room of Mr Li, the proprietor.

The wood-carvers of Hong Kong

6. Ho family garden

in Kowloon City. In its traditional provenience, Ho Ka Yuen must have been a valuable piece of suburban property. The walled city of Kowloon was the site of an office of the traditional magistracy, and a customs house of the Qing empire was located nearby in now-suburban Kowloon T'ong.

In 1963, Heng Lung Co. was established by my boss, Mr. Li, and a fellow Dongyang-county native named Wong, as a partnership. It was housed in a building which had served as a movie studio of the Yau Q Motion picture Co. since shortly after World War II. The movie company, along with two others in the immediate vicinity, oppressed by the spreading noise and clamor of what was becoming the fully urban Kowloon City section of the colony, and by the ever-increasing volume of air traffic using nearby Kai Tak Airport, sold out their interests to seek a greater quiet in the New Territories.

Since that time, Ho Ka Yuen has become a haven for industrial squatting. In defiance of zoning regulations which prohibit construction on tracts of land such as Ho Ka Yuen, which were still zoned as agricultural, a maze of shacks sprang up on the site, and now house plastic flower factories, doll factories, rattan factories, metal shops, a paint factory, a factory producing counterfeit watch faces (to be placed on the mechanisms of cheap Swiss watches and sold as expensive brands) and cubicles that serve in many cases as the homes of whole families.

It is rumored that the government has intentions of clearing the site, and

96

developing the area in a manner similar to that of the surrounding Kowloon City section. Mr Li, who is now the sole proprietor of Heng Lung Co., having bought out his partner in 1966, occupies one of the few registered buildings on the site and will do well in compensation from the government when its intentions to develop Ho Ka Yuen become clear.

During the period of my apprenticeship, my boss did business with five separate shops in the tourist section of Tsimshatsui (see Figure 4). The lion's share of this trade was done with three of these shops, the other two taking only a small part of his business. In addition, he prepared several orders for direct sale or export, but these constituted a very small percentage of the total business transacted while I was there.

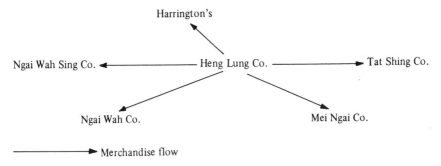

Figure 4. Heng Lung Co.'s trading partners

In a sophisticated *laissez-faire* port like Hong Kong with a long history as an *entrepôt*, one would imagine that business tends to be business (Sillin 1972: 342). One does not expect to find social relations, other than those of pure economic rationality, playing a very large role in the transfer of merchandise and payment. Even in the small city of Lukang, Taiwan, De Glopper found that:

> Businessmen are wary of attempts to utilize particularist relations in business, not only because they may be exploited, but because any special favor received puts one under obligation and thus reduces one's autonomy. . . The businessmen of Lukang stress their own autonomy and freedom of action, and describe business relations as founded on simple economic rationality, with factors of price, quality, and demonstrated reliability taking precedence over ascribed and effective bonds (De Glopper 1969:3).

In Lukang, the business community is, however, homogeneous. 'Outsiders do not settle in Lukang, and everyone there is a native Lukanga, as were his father and grandfather' (De Glopper 1969:8).

Hong Kong differs fundamentally in this respect, it being a city whose population consists almost exclusively of outsiders. Thus while the factors of price, quality and demonstrated reliability are important in the conduct of business in

The wood-carvers of Hong Kong

Hong Kong's free market, ascribed and affective bonds between businessmen are perhaps more important than might be expected, and economically perfectly rational in the Hong Kong context. This was particularly so among small manufacturers of non-Cantonese descent who moved to Hong Kong in the postwar period. It was a relatively small group of Cantonese and pre-war immigrant Shanghainese businessmen, apart from the expatriate British, who were in control of the extensive infrastructure of trade and commercial institutions that Hong Kong had developed in the period before World War II.

In the post-war era, the small non-Cantonese manufacturers, like those from Zhejiang and Shanghai in the art-carved furniture line, made the best possible use of whatever ascribed bonds they could to gain a secure market outlet for their goods amidst a population which was almost exclusively Cantonese. In traditional times, such practices were always employed when Chinese natives of one city, county or province did business in another (Morse 1909:35ff). Associations of merchants who came from the same place were common fixtures in most large towns by Qing dynasty times (Van der Sprenkle 1962:9). They shared the setting with associations of local tradesmen organized according to their special skill or product, like the Merchants' Association we shall meet in the next chapter.

My own boss was a member of the Dongyang *tong xiang hui* (same native place association; see Chapter 4) and his business relations reflected this. The five companies which purchased goods from him during my apprenticeship were all owned by men from Dongyang county. Whether it is because he knew these men in the old country, whether it is because he shares membership with them in the Dongyang association, whether it is because he can speak to them in his native dialect, whether he trusts them because he knows something of their background and history and shares it, whether he can count on their help in times of distress, for whatever reason, he gains something in the way of predictability of the behavior of his business associates in an otherwise alien and highly competitive setting by doing business with his fellow countymen, and is conscious of it.

With several of these Zhejiang business associates relations are particularly cordial. Once a year, my boss and his wife attend a New Year's banquet at Tat Shing Co. Another of his associates owns Ngai Wah Co., with which Heng Lung Co. has a special business relationship. My boss's daughter married the son of the proprietor of Ngai Wah Co., which drew the two families, and the two firms, much closer together. Most of the business done between the in-law firms in the period of my fieldwork was off the record. Heng Lung Co. supplied Ngai Wah Co. with merchandise and was paid for it, but the transaction never appeared on either company's official records. Hence, a little extra profit, on which no taxes had to be paid, was made all round. While the companies had always done business, the marriage between them added a little something extra, and in addition guaranteed the relation in perpetuity. It should be noted, however, that the bulk of my boss's business was not carried on with Ngai Wah Co.

The children have been in the United States for some years and my boss's son-in-law has earned an engineering degree from a prominent American university. In the winter of 1975, in search of a more remunerative occupation, he opened a retail carved-furniture shop on a major downtown Manhattan street, turning Ngai Wah Co. into a virtual multi-national corporation. My surprise could not have been greater when, in December, 1975, I received a phone call from Mr Li, who had flown to New York City to see his daughter, and for the grand opening of the new shop.

De Glopper suggests that cultivation of particularist relations in the conduct of business may be a response to 'uncertainty, or the absence of free access to supplies or markets' (De Glopper 1969:42). Even excluding consideration of the uncertainty of Hong Kong's political future, the total reliance of the port of Hong Kong on imports for its raw materials and machinery, and on exports for sale of its merchandise, introduces a greater degree of uncertainty in the conduct of business than might be expected to prevail in Lukang, Taiwan. As has been mentioned, woods from southeast Asian countries have increased greatly in price. Labor costs have risen and this has made the export price of finished carved-wood products much higher. I ordered a camphorwood chest from my boss for H.K.$450 in 1972, and by the time it was finished and delivered, had I wanted another, I would have had to pay H.K.$600.

In addition, decline in the value of the U.S. dollar beginning in 1972 has meant that the formerly most reliable customers, American importers and tourists, have lost a good deal of their international purchasing power. Shop owners in the tourist section complain that 'they only look, and don't buy'.

While increased demand by Japanese tourists and commercial agents was picking up some of the slack, the art-carved furniture firm had to make considerable adjustments in its commercial relations in order to come through unscathed.

Most factory bosses, therefore, without their own independent marketing capability, maintain business connections with more than one retail outlet for their goods in the tourist section, even if all their associates are same native countymen. This protects them further against market fluctuations and also creates a network throughout the industry, of which my boss and his five business associates are a part (see Figure 5).

Having become aware of this network in the course of my apprenticeship, I tried to obtain the information on survey that would make it possible to construct a map of the entire industry, showing relations of business and flow of goods from company to company. However, information on 'who does business with whom' was considered a trade secret by most bosses, and there is little doubt that even bosses who shared some information with the survey team were not telling it all. It is thus all the more remarkable that from the responses elicited, thirty-eight firms could be incorporated into a map of merchandise flow

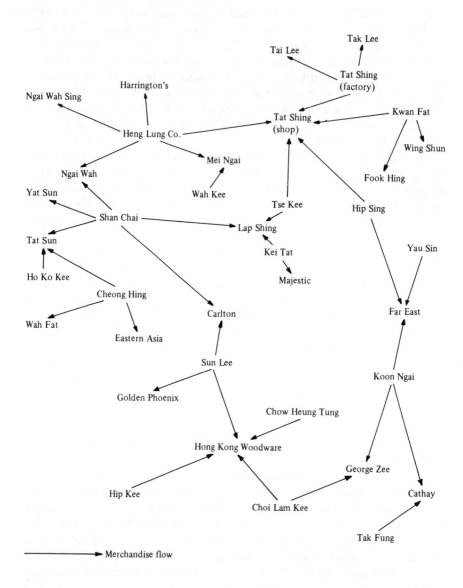

Figure 5. Flow of merchandise in the art-carved furniture industry

that leaves no link broken in the chain (see Figure 5). The interrelatedness of all the factories in the line is clearly demonstrated, and gives concrete expression to the traditional Chinese term descriptive of the community of merchants in the same line of business — *nei hang ren* (see Shiba 1977:416).

100

Commercial relations, structure and practice

One might ask, in view of what has been said about the tendency for natives of the same place of origin to do business together, how such interrelatedness is maintained. It is maintained through the larger firms — companies like Tat Shing, Far Eastern Furnishings and George Zee. Less prone to suffer from the vagaries of market forces, and less in need of guarantees than the small enterprises, these companies do business with all comers and cement the industry together. They act as major funnels for merchandise out of the colony, although all merchandise does not necessarily pass through their hands. They are the kind of organizations which can afford to send agents on promotional tours to the United States, Europe, Japan, Taiwan and southeast Asia to make business contacts there on their own, and they are also the firms who have diversified into modern furniture styles to a very large extent.

The interrelatedness of all the factories and shops in the present-day Hong Kong art-carved furniture industry makes for great ease in starting new business relations. It creates a large number of mutual associates, and the existence of the network might even be viewed as adaptive in a situation where the market for one's goods is relatively uncertain.

A recommendation from an associate can lead to the opening of another line along which one can send one's own merchandise. Such introductions were cited most frequently by respondent shop owners as the way new associates were met. A shop with an excess of orders to fill will rely on such introductions as a simple expedient in multiplying its business contacts, at the same time elaborating the complex network throughout the industry.

One of my boss's associates, Harrington Co., made a rather lucrative arrangement with a firm in Okinawa which required a great deal of merchandise to stock a new business. Harrington's, unable to meet all the orders on its own, passed on its good fortune to my boss, who stood to profit handsomely from a direct line to the expanding Japanese market. This saved him the considerable effort he might otherwise have had to expend in adapting to changing market conditions.

As shops are often clustered on particular streets of the tourist section, one's goods are, in a sense, on display when deliveries are made. On one occasion, when a delivery of my boss's merchandise was made on Canton Road, and the hired truck was being unloaded, a shop owner approached us and inquired about the possibility of buying furniture from Heng Lung Co. Telephone numbers were exchanged and it is possible that the two companies may be doing business at this very moment. Such incidents indicate another way in which the industry-wide network may be elaborated.

The lines along which merchandise flows throughout the industry are also the lines along which credit is alternately given and taken by most bosses in the industry. In the normal course of events in a stable business climate, a factory boss will occupy alternately the roles of creditor and debtor with respect to his marketing outlet, according to a fairly regular rhythm. It would be revealing to be able to construct a map of lines of credit, and their fluctuations over time, between a series of factory bosses and the units through which they market their merchandise, but such data are of an even less public nature than who does business with whom. Only four bosses gave any figures for the amount of credit ever extended, which ranged from several hundred to as much as H.K.$30,000 and it was clear that details regarding the fluctuations over time were just not forthcoming.

In the week-to-week operation of Heng Lung Co., however, the fluctuations in the credit position of the boss were manifest, and may be taken as illustrative of at least one possible pattern; perhaps typical of other factories of similar size.

At Heng Lung Co., the boss makes a separate trip down to the tourist section, several days to a week after delivery, to collect for his goods. He may also collect an advance, on goods not yet delivered, with which to pay his workers and meet operating expenses. When he ultimately delivers the merchandise, he may more than clear his debt, but put off his collection of the balance for several weeks or months until payment may again be required to meet outstanding commitments. He stores his assets with the proprietor of the marketing outlet, collecting amounts over time to meet operating expenses, until he again requires an advance. The advance is made up again in delivered merchandise, and the process begins again. The boss's relationship with his retailer is not unlike the workers' relationship to the boss with respect to advances and repayment, except that the boss is seldom, if ever, in debt to his workers, whereas the retailer may be as often in debt to the boss as the boss is in debt to him. The factory boss may also use his retail business partner as a source of funds with which to supply loans to his workers and, as the middleman, may adjust his accounts with business partners or workers regularly as the situation allows or demands.

The majority of factory and shop bosses characterize their business relations as direct purchase agreements. The provision of goods to retail outlets to be sold on consignment is a rare occurrence, although it is easy to mistake certain instances in which deferred payment agreements are breached and goods repossessed and rerouted to a different market outlet, for consignment relations. In two instances, I accompanied my boss's son on errands dunning for payment for goods already delivered. One case involved a bad check which was redeposited and cleared, and the second involved the repossession of goods already delivered. The former incident involved roughly a thirty-day deferment period, the latter roughly a ninety-day period. De Glopper found the most common periods for deferred payments to be thirty days, with ten days and ninety days the next most common in Lukang, Taiwan. These were manifested in the use of post-dated checks (De Glopper 1969:14), a means of payment also common in Hong Kong. It is reasonable to assume that a similar range of deferred payment periods was characteristic of the Hong Kong art-carved furniture industry. However, in my boss's dealings with his more reliable market outlets, it was equally common for him to receive advances on large orders on which to operate, so that he was just as often 'in debt' to his retailers as they were in debt to him.

Business at Heng Lung Co. could be characterized as on the good side of fair during my apprenticeship. As an apprentice, I participated in the delivery of most of the merchandise produced at Heng Lung during my stay, and I was thus able to monitor fairly closely the value and size of the company's transactions. From mid-October, 1972 to the beginning of April, 1973, I counted H.K.$45,899 worth of merchandise shipped out of Heng Lung Co., and determined that seven more shipments, whose exact monetary values were unobtainable, amounted to roughly another H.K.$12,000. In my original calculations, I assumed that a few shipments were made in my occasional absence, and arrived at a figure of about H.K.$63,000 worth of business for roughly a six-month period. My look into the account books in 1978 confirmed the general range of the figures, but proved that my monitoring had been more accurate than I had imagined. The books indicated H.K.$59,629 worth of business, meaning that I had missed fewer shipments than I had thought, and that my uncompensated figure of H.K.$57,899 was a fairly good estimate. For the purpose of calculation, it will be convenient to use a figure of H.K.$60,000 total sales for the six-month period under study. This is an average of about H.K.$10,000 a month over a period which included the slow month in which the New Year's holiday falls. It is a figure consistent with my boss's sons characterization of his father's business as normally upwards of H.K.$100,000 a year gross earnings.

During each month, I calculated the boss paid an average of seven workers an average of H.K.$800 a month, or roughly H.K.$5,600 a month in wages. For one month coinciding with the New Year, roughly half the workers were absent for the whole month, meaning, that, for one month, only three workers were paid H.K.$800, or H.K.$2,400 total wages. For the remaining five months at H.K. $5,600 a month, H.K.$28,000 in wages were paid out. Adding in the H.K.$2,400 for the other month gives a figure of roughly H.K.$30,400 in wages paid over the six-month period. This is about 50% of the total earnings of H.K.$60,000 for the period, which accords pretty well with figures obtained for percentage composition of business expenses on survey. Wages there constituted 60% of total business *expenses* for the largest number of bosses. Here they constitute 50% of total revenue, a figure not inconsistent with these results.*

Factory bosses indicated that of total expenses, those for raw materials may be expected to be about half that for wages. According to my boss's son, his father tended to scrimp on raw materials, often employing woods of lesser

---

* If business expenses are $1,000 and wages constitute 60% of that figure, then total wages = $600. Total revenue would be expected to be more than total expenses if a business is operating successfully. It stands to reason that $600 will be a smaller percentage of earnings than of expenses. Allowing for a profit margin of 20%, total revenue would be $1,200. If wages account for x% of the revenue, then x = 50%. At Heng Lung Co. this was precisely the percentage of total revenue constituted by wages.

The wood-carvers of Hong Kong

quality. It would therefore make sense to assume a figure of H.K.$10,000 for raw materials over the six-month period. This brings the total expenses so far to H.K.$40,400.

Factory bosses reported that rent, depreciation of capital and other overhead costs amounted to 10% of total expenses in the largest number of cases. Thus the figure H.K.$40,400 can be assumed to represent 90% of my boss's expenses, and total expenses, including overheads, were probably about H.K.$44,900 (rounded to the nearest hundred).

Over the six months then, according to my calculations, my boss made a profit of roughly H.K.$2,500 a month, of which a significant portion was accounted as wages paid by my boss (as boss) to my boss (as a worker in his own factory), thus decreasing the net profit shown.

When I was finally able to consult my boss's account books, I discovered that the actual figure for wages paid out during the six-month period in question was H.K.$39,056, almost H.K.$9,000 more than I had estimated, and almost 65% of the total revenue. If H.K.$10,000 is allowed again for raw materials costs, and H.K.$5,000 for overhead expenses, total expenses come to H.K.$54,000, leaving a profit of H.K.$6,000 for the six-month period or roughly H.K.$1,000 a month.

This last figure is no more than the wages of a worker in the art-carved furniture industry, and would scarcely seem to justify keeping the factory open. If the boss could earn H.K.$1,000 a month as a wage-laboring carpenter, why should he bother with the additional organizational and operational problems of managing a factory with so small an additional payoff?

Two factors seem plausible in accounting for his seemingly small rewards. The first is that his account books seriously understated his earnings deliberately to conceal the profits of his business for tax purposes. Such practices are widespread in Hong Kong, and most businesses keep more than a single set of account books, only one set of which are ever open to inspection for assessment of taxes, or to the inquisitive anthropologist. This explanation of the low-profit figures in the accounts is given a certain credibility by the rather comfortable style of life in which my boss was able to support his family, well above the level that would be possible on the earnings of a wage-laboring carpenter.

He provided an extra share of consumer goods to the household, most notable among which were beer and brandy for himself. He and his wife were able to take a vacation and travel back to their native village in Dongyang county, Zhejiang, a considerable expense. The Li family living room was redecorated in wood paneling and several articles of new furniture were purchased during my stay. The eldest son was supported through college in Canada, and two others have since gone overseas to study. Two daughters are married and living overseas, one a nurse in London, whose training the family supported, and the other a housewife in the United States, whose husband runs the branch of the Ngai Wah Co. furniture business in Manhattan.

Commercial relations, structure and practice

The second factor which seems equally likely is that my boss was finding it increasingly difficult in 1972–3 to realize a profit from his business in the context of rising labor and raw materials costs; that, as a relatively small operation, he was already feeling the competitive pinch from larger, more highly capitalized furniture firms, and the constraints of a price ceiling of products of the Peoples' Republic. Thus, despite his ability to support his family on past earnings and savings, his business in the 1970s may indeed have taken a definite turn for the worse.

Despite the fact that a portion of my boss's accumulated earnings were re-invested in the business to replace old machinery of foreign manufacture, he showed little interest in expanding or diversifying his enterprise. Indeed, as many of his traditional and republican forebears, my boss invested a fair portion of his accumulated earnings in real estate. In Hong Kong, where land is in short supply and the economic climate is uncertain, purchase of real estate remains a safe and popular way to invest one's profits.

The boss owned a flat on Fuk Lo Ts'un Road, where some twenty years ago he ran a carpentry business. When he moved to his present location, he kept possession of the old flat and collects a monthly rental which supplements his income.

During my stay, Mr Li also purchased a flat in a newly constructed high-rise apartment complex in the Tokwawan area, strictly as an income-producing investment. While I am not sure what he paid for it, it could not have cost less than H.K.$15,000, of which perhaps a third was required as down-payment. The flat itself may now be serving as factory premises, if not as a residential apartment. It lies in a noisy industrial neighborhood and would not make comfortable domestic living. Nevertheless, the availability of real estate in Hong Kong is certain to remain scarce, and the value of the flat will never go down. Mr Li stands to do very well in the process.

It is conceivable that he could do even better in the immediate future by reinvesting a greater share of his profits in the expansion and diversification of his business. The traditional practice of reinvestment in land has been noted by economists as a drain on the industrial capital available for economic develop-ment in the traditional and Republican Chinese contexts, as well as in the ex-perience of many countries of the industrializing Third World. For my own boss, the strategy of reinvestment in land may be one reason why his enterprise has not expanded much since its inception fifteen years ago, and may be taken as evidence of a lingering conservatism in business practice. It is clear, however, that there are carved-furniture producers for whom reinvestment in and expansion of their firms has become the rule to a larger extent than for Mr Li. This is particularly so in recent years, when younger family members who have studied business administration abroad have returned home to take over the family businesses (p. 18).

Nevertheless, I do not mean to imply that present-day business conditions

The wood-carvers of Hong Kong

in Hong Kong, and in the art-carved furniture industry in particular, make investment in land totally anachronistic. This is far from the case. Wholly dependent on the vagaries of a world market beyond his control for success in business, the small manufacturer in Hong Kong invests in land as a hedge against uncertain future market conditions.

In the context of a fair business climate with labor and raw materials costs rising, and with the future outlook made uncertain by world economic recession and international currency fluctuations, investment in land might well be characterized as a wise rather than conservative strategy. Land is scarce in Hong Kong and such investment can be recouped quite rapidly. Even the assumed deadline of 1997 has not prevented its widespread popularity.

In the course of the survey, factory bosses and shop owners were asked what factors were most important in making for success in the art-carved furniture industry. The most frequent responses are given in Table 9.

Table 9. *Most frequent responses of factors making for success in the art-carved furniture industry*

Response	Number of occurrences
Maintaining good relations with workers or otherwise ensuring a supply of labor	26
Availability of capital	12
Quality	8
Hard work	7
Experience	6
Consumer demand	5
Stable supply of raw materials	5
Reputation	3
Administrative ability	3
Fair price, quick service, ability to learn	2 each
Stable society, stable currency, location, sincerity, ability to speak English	1 each

What these responses show is the overriding concern of art-carved furniture manufacturers to maintain a stable source of labor as integral to success. It is clear that the skilled labor force of hand manufacture is still a factor to be reckoned with. While the craft character of the product has been undermined by post-1960 developments, the skilled artisan is not yet replaceable completely by semi-skilled or unskilled workers. Increased capital requirements have not yet pushed the division of labor as far as that. The boss must still try to keep his skilled workers happy, and worker—boss relations is an area in which it is well within the power of the individual shop and factory boss directly to affect the efficiency and productivity of his business. Other factors such as stable prices of raw materials or maintaining demand for one's products are often outside his control. It was primarily in an effort to deal systematically with their scarce and temperamental labor supply that the art-carved furniture bosses organized the Merchants' Association in 1960 with which the following chapter will deal in more detail.

Availability of capital, while most important as a factor in starting a business, was significantly less important in achieving success in one's business once it was in operation, at least in comparison with securing one's labor supply. It was mentioned by only twelve bosses. Nevertheless, as the reader is no doubt by now aware, capital is much more important to a contemporary art-carved furniture operation than it was to a similar operation in 1960. No boss in present-day Hong Kong could run an operation competitively without the standard inventory of labor-saving carpentry machines, which are expensive and must be treated and maintained with care.

In the 'manufacture' of certain wares in Republican Chinese treaty ports, capital requirements were so small that newly graduated apprentices, unable to find work as skilled workers, started their own businesses staffed entirely by a new supply of unpaid apprentice labor (Fong & Ku 1935:521). While furniture production was probably somewhat more capital-intensive, even in its period of manufacture, the concentration of ownership of a greatly enlarged inventory of capital equipment, almost exclusively in the hands of the boss, is a phenomenon which has only made its appearance over the past fifteen years. Capital is today more of a factor making for success than ever before, in spite of the bosses' still heavy reliance on skilled labor.

The next most frequently mentioned factor making for success was quality, mentioned eight times. This is rather surprising in view of my own experience at Heng Lung Co., where it was explained to me that producing greater quantities of cheaper ware nets a greater long-term profit than producing lesser quantities of special-order pieces on which a great deal of care is lavished. There is an upper limit on the time spent per item produced, beyond which the returns for extra labor inputs do not match the returns to be gained from beginning a second item with the same portion of labor time. In spite of the fact that speed and quantity of output were not often mentioned by the bosses as factors in success, it seems to me that these variables are considerably more important than quality in the success equation. The scramble for competitive advantage in the highly uncertain climate of Hong Kong's free market has led to a general decline in quality of Hong Kong made art-carved furniture. The taking of quick profits, high rates of capital turnover, small shelf stocks and production at top speed make sense in the economic setting, which is also conducive to selection of business associates from fellow provincials, the consolidation of business relations through marriage, membership in same native place associations, and investment in real estate.

In spite of the fact that most factory bosses claimed that the quality of their goods was superior to that of other Hong Kong art-carved furniture factories, it is my impression that quality varies little from factory to factory in Hong Kong. As workers have little sense of loyalty to the firm in which they work, a boss is hard put to assemble and maintain a work force that is markedly superior in skill to that of any other factory in Hong Kong. The same workers are found producing goods at many different factories in the course of their careers, and this makes for a rather uniform quality from firm to firm throughout the industry. Quality can be obtained by the consumer for a price, but must be demanded, and paid for at a level sufficient to compensate for the labor time which could be devoted to the production and sale of another lesser quality item. It is probable that bosses' responses regarding the superior quality of their own merchandise represented an attempt to get in a little free advertising. As no factory boss admitted that his wares were of poorer quality than those of other Hong Kong firms, this reasoning seems sound.

Fewer factory bosses entertained any illusions about how their goods matched up to those of Mainland Chinese manufacture, produced under conditions in which most factors of production are rigorously controlled. While the price ceiling established by the higher quality Chinese product has risen in recent years, it has done so in response to factors that have little to do with the conditions in Hong Kong which are responsible for rising production costs. The entrance of Chinese carved-wood products into the world 'free' (U.S.) market gives that price ceiling a greater significance to Hong Kong manufacturers than ever before, making their competitive position all the more precarious.

The art-carved furniture manufacturer has two alternatives, both of which mean a further undermining of the traditional craft skills which were maintained in a regime of manufacture', and which, to a lesser degree, still prevail in the industry today. The first entails accentuating the drive for fast profits with high rates of capital turnover, so as not to be caught with too much capital invested into one's business, should the price ceiling be breached and the Hong Kong manufacturer be forced out of business. The second entails a further movement toward greater capitalization and diversification out from under the price ceiling established by Mainland Chinese carved-wood furniture.

The success of the first strategy is of course contingent on the compliance of labor, a factor upon which the art-carved furniture manufacturers cannot at the moment conveniently rely. The Merchants' Association in its present state cannot guarantee it. The second strategy therefore seems more likely to prevail.

7

The Merchants' Association

The Hong Kong Kowloon Art-Carved Furniture and Camphorwood Chests Merchants' Association (the Merchants' Association) came into existence in its present form in 1960, when, as has been pointed out, income divisions between boss and worker were growing progressively wider, the market for carved-wood products was reaching a saturation point and a labor force which had remained quiescent for about ten years began to agitate with greater vigor. With little further prospect for expansion of production in the carved-furniture curio market, and workers demanding a larger share of the profits, art-carved furniture manufacturers united in defense of their common interests.

Merchants' associations of a similar type had existed in the art-carved furniture industry prior to World War II in the ports of Hong Kong, Canton and Shanghai. There the merchandise was 'manufactured' in a setting in which guilds had been abandoned by worker members for labor unions, leaving behind them the factory owners who, in certain instances, remained unorganized, or, where it suited their interests, established merchants' associations of factory and shop owners of the trade.

In Hong Kong, a merchants' association in the then primarily camphor-wood chests industry was first organized in 1938. The first vice-chairman of that association recounts how it was organized to secure supplies of necessary camphorwood when sources along the West River of Guangdong province previously obtained at Hu Men were cut off by Japanese activities in the area. Some supplies were still available in and around Canton Bay and the manufacturers of camphorwood chests organized an association to assure that supplies would continue to enter the colony of Hong Kong. Located then on Johnston Road on Hong Kong island, the association lasted only till 1941 when Japanese occupation of Hong Kong brought the industry to a stand-still. Large numbers of Hong Kong residents fled the colony at that time to return to their native villages in Guangdong, where sources of food were somewhat more reliable. Workers and bosses of the still relatively small camphor-wood chests industry of Hong Kong were among them. Those who stayed on in Hong Kong did their best to scrape through in other occupations.*

After the war, in 1948–9, an attempt was made to reorganize the association, but business was poor and few bosses had sufficient funds to support an association's existence. There was little enthusiasm for the effort and the attempt failed. The large numbers of refugee businessmen who entered the colony after 1949 were not to find an association necessary for the more than ten years of expansive 'manufacturing' activity which were to follow.

Capital accumulation proceeded smoothly until saturated markets and labor agitation prompted the formation of the Merchants' Association of the art-carved furniture industry in its present form. In a great rush of enthusiasm fully 111 firms of Cantonese and Shanghainese capital, in rosewood and teak/camphor-wood lines, joined together in the effort and formulated the goals of the Merchants' Association as follows:

1 To mediate disputes between member and member or member and workers.
2 To promote and maintain the well-being of merchants and manufacturers of this trade.
3 To investigate and study advantages and disadvantages in solving problems of this trade.
4 To comply with, maintain, or oppose (as appropriate) laws or any other arrangements relating to this trade either in this colony or elsewhere.
5 To translate or explain the laws or ordinances of industrial trade announced by the Hong Kong government or by the governments of other countries and to circulate them to all members for reference.
6 To compile statistics and publish information concerning this trade.
7 To examine and check on the condition, quality or source of merchandise and issue certificates of authenticity (important under the terms of the U.S. trade embargo which forbade the import to the United States of goods made in Communist China or of Communist Chinese materials).
8 To obtain raw materials for the purpose of adequately supplying the needs of members.
9 To study reforms of production and technique of this trade to meet present-day requirements.
10 To develop international markets for export and to maintain contact with all commercial organizations which might arrange or promote business of the members.
11 To assist members in settling difficult problems involving either finance, production or business and to seek legal advice.
12 To protect the rights of members and to draw up trade regulations for this industry.
13 To issue newspapers, journals, magazines, booklets, or other publications to promote and propagate the aims, purposes and principles of this association.
14 To hold exhibitions of the products of this trade.

* For more information on this period, see Lethbridge (1969) and Luff (1967). For a rather slanted version by an indignant expatriate Britisher, see Carew (1960).

15 To establish welfare works such as schools, entertainment centers, clinics, etc.

16 To promote scientific management of workshops or factories, to establish training classes in production techniques, commercial advertising, international business, sales promotion; to create a reserve of capable manpower to advance our business.

17 To hold an entertainment meeting twice a year, once in Spring, once in Autumn to increase good friendship and strengthen the unity among all members.

18 To encourage those legal organizations which aim to promote the interests of this trade.

(Merchants' Association 1963)

There is no question that the Merchants' Association had a clear notion of what was required to serve its members' immediate future interests, and its leadership set about securing for its membership a means of promoting those interests in the highest reaches of the Hong Kong political and business community. Through the creation of an Honorary Advisory Board, the new Merchants' Association consolidated an important channel of communication through to some of the most important and influential individuals in the colony. The commercial network, described in the previous chapter as encompassing virtually the entire art-carved furniture industry, was thereby linked to circles of economic and political power which dwarfed the entire network by comparison. The Association made it possible to mobilize on its members' behalf, should it become necessary, the power of such Honorary Advisory Board members as the following:

Honorary President *Ngan Shing-Kwan* — born in Hong Kong 1905, a follower of Sun Yat-sen, appointed Commander Order of the British Empire, 1932; Justice of the Peace; Unofficial Member Executive Council and Senior Member Legislative Council; Unofficial Member of Urban Council 1946–1953; Founder and Managing Director China Motor Bus Co. Ltd.; Public Transport Advisory Committee 1951–1958; Hong Kong delegate to the Eighth Session of Economic Council on Asia and the Far East (E.C.A.F.E.), Rangoon, 1952; Seventh Session of E.C.A.F.E. Committee of Industry and Trade, Tokyo, 1955; Principal delegate to the Eighth Session of E.C.A.F.E. Committee of Industry and Trade, Bangalore, India, 1956; Chairman of Directors, Liu Chong Hing Bank, Ltd.; Director of the Hong Kong Chinese Bank, Ltd.; Member Board of Education; the Court of the University of Hong Kong; Board of Governors, Ch'ung Ch'i College; Board of Trustees True Light Middle School; Board of Trustees United College; Chinese Permanent Cemetery Board of Management; Chinese Temples Committee; Chinese Recreation Ground Committee; Deputy Chairman of Hong Kong Subsidiary Branch of the Commonwealth Parliamentary Association; Director Repulse Bay Enterprises, Ltd.; Wong Hing Lung Co.; President Chiu Chow Residents' Association; Chairman of the Hong Kong Kowloon Chiu Chow School Council; First Chairman Board of Directors Tung Wah Group of Hospitals — 1931; Po Leung Kuk — 1939; Chiu Chow Chamber of Commerce; Chairman

The wood-carvers of Hong Kong

Alice Ho Miu Ling Nethersole Hospital – 1956–1957; Chairman Board of Directors Tai-Kwong Newspaper and Printing Co. Ltd; Chairman Ka Wah Life Assurance Co.; Director New Asia Hotels – 1934; Member District Watch Committee – 1931, 1942.

(See Rear (1971a) for an explanation of many of the positions; Lethbridge (1969) for a discussion of the activities of the District Watch Committee, Tung Wah Group of Hospitals and other honorary prestigious positions.)

Honorary President *C. L. Hsu* — born Zhejiang 1901; Chairman and Managing Director Diaward Steel Works, Ltd.; Permanent Director Hong Kong Chinese Bank, Ltd.; The Far Eastern Insurance Co. Ltd.; Former Chairman Relief Section, Chinese Rehabilitation Advisory Committee of the Hong Kong Government; Principal Director Tung Wah Group of Hospitals 1947–1948; Vice-Chairman Chinese Manufacturers' Association; First President and Founder Lion's Club of Hong Kong; Former Chairman Hong Kong Enamelware Manufacturers' Association; First Chairman Happy Valley and Canal Road District Kaifong Welfare Association; Chairman Jiangsu/Zhejiang Association, 1949–1966; Chairman Hong Kong Aluminiumware Manufacturers' Association; Chairman School Council Jiangsu/Zhejiang College; Director Aluminium Manufacturing Co. Hong Kong Ltd.; Honorary President Chinese Manufacturers' Association, 1954–1966.

Honorary Advisors to the Merchants' Association included *Paul Tsui*, former Secretary of Chinese Affairs (now Home Affairs) Department of the Hong Kong Government. In 1972–3 Mr Tsui was also Commissioner of Labor and member of the Legislative Council.

A second Honorary Advisor was:

The Honourable Sir *J. D. Clague* – born 1917 Rhodesia; Knight; Military Cross, 1942; OBE (Military) 1943; CBE (Military) 1946; Appointed Unofficial Justice of the Peace 1952; Member Executive Council; Chairman the Federation of Hong Kong Industries; Member Urban Council 1952–1959; President Hong Kong Family Welfare Society; Chairman Hong Kong Housing Society; Hong Kong Police Commandant, Auxiliary Police Force; Hong Kong War Memorial Fund Committee; Grantham Scholarship Fund Committee; Transport Advisory Committee; Director John D. Hutchison and Co. Ltd.; Hutchison (Building) Ltd.; Hutchison (Finance) Ltd.; The Hong Kong and Shanghai Banking Corp.; Mercantile Bank Ltd.; British Traders Insurance Co. Ltd.; North Pacific Insurance Co. Ltd.; Wheelock Marden and Stewart, Ltd.; The American Engineering Corp. Fed. Inc. U.S.A.; American Lloyd Travel Service Ltd; Cross Harbour Tunnel Co. Ltd.; The Dairy Farm Ice and Cold Storage Co. Ltd.; Asian Food Industries Hong Kong Ltd.; Far Eastern Motors, Ltd.; Eastern Motors Ltd.; Turin Motors Ltd.; Harrimans (Harriman Realty Co.) Ltd.; The Hong Kong and China Gas Co. Ltd.; International Engineering Ltd.; Carnes and Co. Ltd.; Hong Kong Realty and Trust Co. Ltd.; Muirleaf Trading Corp. Ltd.; Associated Holdings Ltd.; Oriental Mortgage and Finance Corp. Ltd.; Precast Products Ltd.; Property Development (Industrial) Ltd.; F. E. Skinner (Hong Kong) Ltd.; Shewan Tomes (Equipment) Ltd.; Realty Development Co. Ltd.;

The Merchants' Association

World Wide (Shipping) Ltd.; Chairman of Directors Hutchison International, Ltd.; Hutchison International Insurance Agency Ltd.; Blair and Co. Ltd.; John Cowie & Co. Ltd.; Coolants Ltd.; Davie Boag & Co. Ltd.; L. Dunbar & Co. Ltd.; Gordon Woodroffe and Co. (Far East) Ltd.; Hong Kong Oxygen and Acetylene Co. Ltd.; Inurs and Riddle (China) Ltd.; Liddell Bros. & Co. Ltd.; Oriental Pacirif Mills Ltd.; Reiss Bradley & Co. Ltd.; Robertson Wilson & Co. Ltd.; Shewan Tomes (Trading) Ltd.; Steward, the Royal Hong Kong Jockey Club (Rear 1971a:126–7).

The Honorary Auditor, Mr *Thomas LeC. Kuen*, is listed in *Prominent Chinese of Hong Kong* (1937) as the proprietor of the first and only Chinese incorporated accountant and auditor practice in Hong Kong. He is the son of Lee Gockchew, a director of Wing On Co. Ltd, a Chinese owned conglomerate dating from Republican times, with holdings in department stores, banks, insurance, etc.

Lastly although not an honorary officer, Sir *Chau Tsun-nin*, officiated at one of the early swearing-in ceremonies of the officers of the Merchants' Association. Sir Chau's list of credentials is also impressive:

Sir *Chau Tsun-nin* – born Hong Kong 1893; Knight; C.B.E.; Ll.D.; Order of St. John; J.P. 1923; Unofficial Member Legislative Council 1931–1953; Unofficial Member Executive Council 1946–1959; Director Hong Kong Electric Co. Ltd.; Hong Kong Telephone Co. Ltd.; Hong Kong and Yaumati Ferry Co. Ltd.; Hong Kong Shipyard Ltd.; Wo Shing Co.; You On Shipping Co. Ltd.; Managing Director Chun On Fire Insurance Co. Ltd.; Hinson Co. Ltd.; Director American Pacific Life Insurance Co. Ltd.; The China Emporium Ltd.; Allied Investors Corp. Ltd.; Property Development (Industrial) Ltd.; Hong Kong and Far Eastern Investment Co. Ltd.; Member St. John Council for Hong Kong; St. John Ambulance Association and Brigade; Vice-Member of the Committee, Alice Ho Miu Ling Nethersole Hospital.*

A more awesome display of Hong Kong Chinese capital and influence could hardly be assembled. The presence of Sir Douglas Clague serves to include the upper echelons of the expatriate British community as well. The circle in which such gentlemen interact on a day-to-day basis is seldom breached by the art-carved furniture manufacturer. While one or another of such manufacturers occasionally makes the jump to the fringes of this elite Hong Kong community, such as the current Chairman of the Merchants' Association, who sits on the board of the Tung Wah Group of Hospitals and is a Lions Club Member, the large majority of association members content themselves with a comfortable living far below the standards of Hong Kong's elite. Indeed, most furniture manufacturers of the early 1960s could only dream of success measured in such terms.

As might be expected, these illustrious figures of the Hong Kong political

* Except where otherwise noted, all the above compilations come from the *Hong Kong Directory*, 1961 and 1973; *Hong Kong Album*, 1961 and 1966; and *Prominent Chinese of Hong Kong*, 1937 (ed. S. L. Woo).

and economic scene play no role in the week-to-week functions of the Merchants' Association, and only occasionally grace the Association with their presence at yearly functions. Their honorary positions are only that: honorary. Several have had no contact with the Merchants' Association for the more than fifteen years since its original founding. In none of the sources consulted on the backgrounds of any of these gentlemen were their honorary positions in the Merchants' Association even listed. Their appointment to the Honorary Advisory Board of the Association can be seen as nothing more than a recognition of the positions of power they already held in the business community of Hong Kong. The honor thus conferred certainly contributed little extra in terms of the enormous prestige already enjoyed by these gentlemen.

Nevertheless, the honorary status conferred on them by the Merchants' Association placed upon them the subtle obligation to come to the Association's aid in time of need and served to give the Association's members 'call' on a number of potentially influential spokesmen for their interests in the highest levels of government and business at a time when those interests most needed protection.

I have no evidence that these spokesmen were ever mobilized directly to speak for the community of art-carved furniture manufacturers, but on one occasion during my stay, the Merchants' Association formed the organizational locus for an appeal to government on behalf of a group of its members, in which it is conceivable that friends in high places provided the crucial margin of difference in winning a number of concessions for this small group of manufacturers whose very existence was threatened. The incident deserves detailed discussion.

The trouble started when the Hong Kong government announced its intention to clear a portion of land just south of Austin Road in Kowloon, upon which the Whitfield Barracks of the English Armed Forces were situated, and on the borders of which a number of art-carved furniture as well as other small family-run businesses were located. The government intended to lease the barracks land to the Tsimshatsui neighborhood Welfare Association, of which the Merchants' Association Chairman was also an officer, to build and operate a school, and had resumed control over the site in 1967 when the barracks were vacated in a major British troop reduction. The land previously occupied by the English troops thus passed under control of the Hong Kong government in 1967.

Around the army base there had grown up a host of small factories doing contract work of various kinds for the soldiers. Among these were a considerable number of art-carved furniture factories. Some had retail shops on adjoining Canton Road, and others did a brisk business with these same shops and with the barracks soldiers until their departure in 1967. In 1973 there were still 39 factories of various types, 29 families, and in all about 500 people whose livelihood was tied up with the land adjoining Whitfield Barracks.

The factories were technically squatting on *army* land and had been doing so since 1947. The Hong Kong government undertook a squatter survey in 1964, during which all people squatting on *Crown* land were registered, and all such people were thereby entitled to resettlement by the government in government residential and/or factory blocks, should they be forced to vacate their premises. Anyone moving into a squatter area after 1964 was not so entitled.

Unfortunately for the residents of the Whitfield Barracks area, when the registration of squatters occurred in 1964, their land was still under the jurisdiction of the English Armed Forces and the Hong Kong government did not enter the area to register them. When the land reverted to Hong Kong government control in 1967, they became subject to immediate removal and because they had not been registered in 1964, they were technically not entitled to government resettlement or compensation of any kind to replace their homes and businesses.

On June 20, 1973, the government posted notices throughout the area, ordering all occupants to vacate by August 20, 1973. With no prospect for resettlement or even for a temporary move to a government-registered squatter area, many of the factory owners faced the possibility of great losses, with no roof under which to store their machinery and stock. It was a pretty dismal time for the group.

I was first informed of the problem by the Chairman of the Merchants' Association on July 4, 1973, when I went to his shop to pick up some materials he had earlier promised me. He encouraged me to attend a meeting to be held that night by the Whitfield squatters.

The meeting was chaired by the Merchants' Association Vice-Chairman who also had a factory on the threatened site. The problem was explained in detail and a summary was written by the Merchants' Association Secretary and included in a press statement to the Chinese-language newspapers. I was asked to write a letter on the squatters' behalf to the English-language newspapers. The squatters were determined to stay until their case was reviewed by the appropriate government authorities.

It is not clear whether the influence of the Association's Honorary Board Members was mobilized, or if the government authorities were otherwise impressed by the unusual predicament of the Whitfield squatters. In any event, the upshot of the campaign was to win for the squatters a month's extension on the order to quit their premises, and ultimately an offer of resettlement in government resettlement factory blocks in Tsuen Wan, New Territories. Most of the factory owners were quite pleased with this arrangement. While some held out for resettlement nearer the original site, they soon accepted the government's terms as well.

What is important to note is that the Merchants' Association had succeeded in winning a rather valuable prize in the Hong Kong context for a group of its members (and non-members) which otherwise had nowhere near the resources or contacts necessary to plead a case before government. That the association chose not to pursue the case on behalf of those unsatisfied with the initial government offer was really only a question of tactics. The Association clearly acted as a guardian of its members' interests and provided an appropriate channel by means of which its membership could make their interests felt in the highest reaches of government.

It is noteworthy that traditional Chinese guilds served similar functions in the towns and cities in which they operated. They linked manufacturers to the local magistracy through the intermediary of the guild secretary, usually a lettered scholar whose literary training put him on almost equal terms with the local magistrate (Morse 1909:37). Guilds collected taxes from their members for payment to the imperial government (Kato 1936:69) and organized yearly labor services which its members owed to the imperial bureaucracy (MacGowan 1888–9:173). They even maintained courts, which were often recognized as legitimate enforcers of the law by the ruling imperial bureaucracy (Van der Sprenkle 1962:95), and in certain cases the guilds were the only regulators of urban affairs at the town and small city level.

The art-carved furniture industry is not a major economic bastion of the Hong Kong economy and its member firms have never been in a position to oversee community affairs within, let alone outside, their own bailiwick. However, since its inception, it has attempted to keep lines of communication open to the upper echelons of political and economic power of Hong Kong, and in this respect its actions and structural position may be characterized as similar to that of traditional guilds.

In its early years, despite an immediate decline in membership from 111 firms in 1960 to 59 firms in 1961, the Merchants' Association maintained a fairly high level of activity on its members' behalf, which reached a climax in 1964 when it successfully broke the back of the strike of that year (see pp. 75–6). Not surprisingly, its membership figures for 1964 were the highest for any year since the Association's original founding (see Table 10).

In the post-1964 period, however, active and creative programs designed to promote the interests of its members largely ceased. The enthusiasm which had surrounded the first several projects actively initiated by the Merchants' Association seemed spent. Much of the Association's initial promise went unfulfilled.

Among the activities of its early years in which enthusiasm for the Merchants' Association, its goals and its future were manifest, but which never fulfilled their potential, was the purchase of the Association's current premises on Jordan Road in 1962. These consist of a room some 600–700 feet square, decorated modestly with two groups of desks, two sofas, an end table stacked with photo albums in which photos of past functions are pasted, and a long meeting table, surrounded with folding chairs, stretching the length of the room. On the wall, hang two elaborately carved wooden plaques bearing the shield and coat of arms of the Merchants' Association. Encased in one wall are plaques of marble of various sizes, each with a picture and the position in the Association of one of its founding members. The size of the plaque and the picture vary in

116

Table 10. *Membership figures of the Hong Kong Kowloon Art-Carved Furniture and Camphorwood Chests Merchants' Association*

Year	Member firms	Year	Member firms	Year	Member firms
1960	111	1966	64	1972	65
1961	59	1967	63	1973	63
1962	68	1968	56	1974	61
1963	74	1969	42	1975	41
1964	77	1970	63	1976	42
1965	60	1971	64	1977	46

accordance with the contribution made by the member towards the purchase of the premises in 1962.

In a real sense the acquisition of the flat can be said to have given social reality to the Merchants' Association as such, since it bound all members in shares of a common piece of property. It made them a corporate group, and this important event was given coverage in the Chinese press at the time. Sir J. Douglas Clague of Hutchison International officiated.

However, the enthusiasm with which the opening of the headquarters was surrounded died down quickly. Apart from the rather abstract function the flat performs as a mechanism of solidarity, it was of little practical use to its members in the years that were to follow its grand opening. While its monetary value may have quadrupled since the time it was purchased, it remains unused between the Association's infrequent meetings, and only a caretaker is present, seldom bothered by anything except the responsibility of opening mail.

Unlike the premises of the Woodwork Carvers' Union, or even the Dongyang *tong xiang hui*, the Merchants' Association headquarters never became a center for extra-curricular activity. The goals written out as official, such as the provision of schools, training classes, etc., remain unfulfilled. The flat continues its empty existence, a vacant storehouse of the solidarity purchased by its members in 1962 as any other commodity might have been purchased in Hong Kong's free market.

In 1963, the Merchants' Association took its first and last action to promote the sale of carved-wood furniture, whose exports had fallen off since the H.K. $1.64 million high point of 1960. It published a promotional booklet for distribution to potential overseas buyers, extolling the virtues of the products of its member firms through pictures, advertisements and lists of the names and addresses of its member firms. It was an effort to establish a broader market for the carved curio pieces on which the industry's pre-1960 prosperity was founded. Copies of this same booklet were still available in 1973, although more than ten years out of date. Many of the addresses of member firms, where the firms still

117

existed, had changed several times since 1963, and most available copies of the booklet were yellowing with age.

If export figures for carved-wood furniture in the years following the publication of the booklet may be taken as an index of the success of the promotional effort, it was not very successful. The advantage of hindsight allows one to see that diversification into more modern styles held greater expansionary promise in the mid-1960s than attempts to broaden the market artificially for carved curio furniture, especially after the introduction of power-driven machinery. Indeed, it was the firms who adopted the diversification strategy in the mid to late 1960s which were most successful in continuing to expand their enterprises' business.

The Merchants' Association played no active role in promoting either the adoption of machinery or encouraging diversification among its members, despite the fact that such a role was not inconsistent with its goals. Goal number 9, for example, stated that the Merchants' Association hoped to be able to study reforms of production and technique in the trade to meet present-day requirements. This goal went unfulfilled and had serious consequences.

Individual factory and shop proprietors were left to their own devices to improve production technique or diversify into new styles. Those who succeeded competitively owed nothing of their success to the Merchants' Association and nowadays most such bosses consider it a relatively 'useless' organization. Some of the more successful of these have enlarged their businesses to such an extent that they need not be bound by Merchants' Association agreements. They can offer higher wages than the smaller firms to attract scarce workers, and can more easily absorb wage increases, since such increases represent a smaller percentage of their total invested capital. They are also less vulnerable to the price ceiling established by higher quality Mainland Chinese carved furniture, because of their larger volume of sales of less elaborately carved modern pieces turned out in a more highly capitalized and elaborated division of labor.

Having diversified into modern furniture, they are no longer beholden to the Merchants' Association which has so far not made any concerted effort to woo such firms into its membership. In Hong Kong's free market setting of extensive reliance on overseas markets, the Association has been unable to impose any sanctions on firms for not joining the Association or not abiding by its agreements, since the firms in question are the companies most able to market their own merchandise through their own agents overseas.

Unlike the guilds of old, the Merchants' Association is unable to monopolize the trade of its members. The competitive free market conditions of twentieth-century Chinese treaty ports linked to overseas export markets, which undermined the monopoly power of the guilds, persist in *laissez-faire* Hong Kong. Associations like the Merchants' Association are in no position to control prices effectively, to set uniform standards of quality, to levy fines or to boycott recalcitrant businessmen out of business if they refuse to yield to pressure put upon them, as the guilds of old China were reputed to have been able to do (Van der Sprenkle 1962:92–4).

The inability of the Merchants' Association to impose sanctions on its members is clearly illustrated in the following anecdote of my experiences as an apprentice.

Concern was voiced in the trade, that as a non-Chinese, learning the wood-carving craft I would, upon return to the west, teach the skills widely, create a pool of skilled western carvers, and thereby destroy the monopoly of the techniques and production of art-carved furniture enjoyed by Chinese (Hong Kong) producers. It was rumored that the Merchants' Association would soon ask my boss to dispense with my services. Such action would have been entirely consistent with what is known of traditional Chinese guilds which were quite exclusive in their labor recruitment (see Chapter 2; see also Hsü & Ho (1945) on the buthcers' guild of West Town). Indeed, I had found it difficult to secure an apprenticeship on several previous occasions for precisely such reasons.

When my boss raised the subject with me, I told him that I really did not want to cause him any trouble and that if my presence was going to constitute a real inconvenience to him, I would go. His response was simple enough:

I'm in business! I do business with whom I please. I don't do business with the Merchants' Association. [He was nevertheless a member in good standing.] If they want to denounce me, I don't care. What difference does it make? Can they stop me from doing business? No! You let me worry about the Merchants' Association.

Clearly the value of my presence as an English teacher for his son, if not my uncompensated labor in his factory, was greater than the inconvenience of having to deal with any pressure being put upon him. He was in any case certain he could handle it without endangering his livelihood in *laissez-faire* Hong Kong. As it turned out, the Merchants' Association sanctions on my boss never came to more than unofficial mutterings on the part of only a few members, and the Association never considered taking an official stance against my presence, although, even if they had, my boss was well aware of their inability to force him to comply.

What was of great interest to me among the Association's stated goals, the compilation of statistics on the trade, also went unfulfilled in the highly competitive climate of post-war Hong Kong. With no enforcement power, the Association could hardly collect information from bosses concerning their business in an atmosphere where one's business is seldom openly discussed. No Association member would place in the hands of another member even the most simple statistical summary of his yearly business, and I know that the Association never made any attempt to compile any figures at all.

Now this contrasts strikingly with a report by MacGowan in which the proceedings of Chinese guilds, by which sums are assessed for the maintenance of the guild, are described. MacGowan states:

The wood-carvers of Hong Kong

Inquisitorial proceedings like those adopted by [Chinese] guilds to ascertain amounts at which members should be assessed for the maintenance of the institution are certainly remarkable. *In no other land would merchants submit to an examination of their books*, yet in no other land is the mercantile character possessed of greater prescience and acumen. The system is made to work satisfactorily, which is evident from the fact that it is self imposed.

There appears to be some friction in its working attempts being sometimes made to represent current sales as less than the truth warrants. Punishment is provided against delinquents by the infliction of fines (MacGowan 1885—6: 140, emphasis added).

In post-war Hong Kong, the Chinese furniture merchant takes his place along with the merchants in all other lands to which MacGowan alludes. With no power to inflict fines, the Merchants' Association is in no position to extract truthful figures from its members, and charges a fixed fee for membership and yearly dues. Indeed, it is my impression that so odious is the thought of opening one's books to scrutiny today, that the friction which MacGowan noted even in 1885 may have been more serious than he or the guilds were aware.

The state of disregard into which the Merchants' Association has fallen in the eyes of many of its members was evident to a great extent, when in 1973 it granted a 25% increase to the striking communist union without a struggle. Its ability to negotiate vigorously with the ever-recalcitrant scarce skilled workers of the art-carved furniture industry has certainly been undermined, as divisions in the labor force which characterized hand manufacture have for the most part receded into the background. The consolidation by the communist Woodwork Carvers' Union of its leadership of this labor force has certainly not helped.

One boss asked me, 'What good is the Merchants' Association? The workers ask for a raise and they give it without even a fight. Might just as well not have one!' This particular boss stuck to his guns and refused to grant his workers the raise agreed upon in 1973. His factory was promptly emptied of workers, and from that point onward he concentrated strictly on retail sales.

Even the responsibility of policing the industry and issuing Labor Department certificates of origin to its members has become anachronistic. Since the early 1950s, when the U.S. trade embargo on Communist Chinese goods was initiated, all Hong Kong manufacturers required a certificate of origin guaranteeing that their merchandise was not a product or made from products of the Peoples' Republic of China, before any of it could be exported to the United States. The *de facto* lifting of that embargo since approximately 1972 has all but done away with the necessity of this Merchants' Association activity.

Bosses who remain loyal to the Association probably do so more for the occasional opportunities it affords for social interaction with their fellow shop and factory proprietors, than for any immediate economic advantages which it can provide. Business at meetings is usually quickly dispensed with, and all

120

present adjourn to a restaurant to eat, drink and talk, and often to play mah-jong. Characteristically, most members arrive an hour or so late, so as to have as little to do with the actual conduct of business as possible, but as much to do with the post-meeting socializing.

The H.K.$150 a year membership dues earns the member boss a framed plaque stating that he is a fully fledged member of the Association, and the privilege that goes with it of attending the entertainment meetings which are among the only activities of the Association that occur with anything approaching regularity. One of these meetings takes place on the birthday of the craft founder, *Luban* (see Plate 5).

The Merchants' Association prides itself on being a repository of traditional lore concerning woodcarving and furniture production, and encourages its members to think of themselves as the descendants of the great Chinese craftsmen of old. The festivities at the Luban temple in Kennedy Town on the anniversary of the date of birth of the craft founder, and a banquet hosted at a restaurant on the same evening, are the highpoint of social activity during the year. Participation in the ceremonial reverence of the founder of the craft is conscientiously observed, and in the promotional pamphlet of 1963, the Association self-consciously took upon itself the responsibility of compiling and disseminating for its members the extant myths and stories told about the craft founder, Luban, as a means of instilling pride in carrying on the great artistic traditions of past generations of Chinese artisans (see Burgess 1928:185).

I have translated their accounts as follows:

Master Luban was born in 507 B.C. This year (1962) is the 2,468th anniversary of his birth. He was not only the outstanding civil engineer of that period, but was also a specialist in military matters, metal work, and mechanics.

Lubans real name was Gong Xuban, or Gong Xuzu. He was from the state of Lu (Shandong of today) of the Spring and Autumn period (722–481 B.C.). Since he was respected by members of all classes, he was given the name of the state of Lu, and he was called Luban.

He was born in the reign of Lu Ding-gong at the end of Spring and Autumn period. His family had been involved in non-agricultural occupations for generations and he too became a technician talented at invention. He was extremely skillful and later generations, revering his near god-like abilities, deified him in the more than 2,000 years that followed. According to traditional stories, Luban not only excelled in building houses, but also in boat-building and cart-building, and he is even said to have invented a kite-like wooden airplane.

According to the ancient books, the state of Chu was continually at war and needed people to make armaments. Knowing of Luban's excellence in technical design, they sent people with many gifts to invite him to come to Chu.

At Chu, he invented a long ladder to attack city walls. Chu used the ladder to good advantage, and it was to become a powerful weapon in Chu's attack and victory over Song. This story appears historically in the works of Mo-tzu who said 'Song was conquered after the ladder of Gong Xuban was built'.

Luban also invented a wooden kite for the state of Chu which was very much like a wooden airplane. The Hung book says, 'Gong Xuban made a wooden kite to spy on Song'. This kite could carry a man aloft and was not unlike today's reconnaissance planes in its capabilities. In fact, more than 2,000 years ago, this kite worked on principles similar to modern-day gliders. According to stories among the people, this wooden kite could stay up in the air for three days at a time.

It is said that Luban at one time rode the kite for more than 1,000 *li* to see his wife for whom he was feeling lonesome and returned within the day. It is also said that Luban himself realized the great military significance of this invention for the future.

When Chu invaded Yue, Luban invented a kind of grappling hook, a weapon for amphibious fighting. When Chu attacked, they used the hook to advance, and when they were forced to retreat, they could easily release it. The result was that Chu soldiers defeated Yue decisively.

It is said that Luban's father was killed by the people of the state of Wu and he wanted to avenge his father's death. He built a wooden idol south of the wall of Xiu, the idol's hand pointing south. The state of Wu suffered drought for three years. Finally the people of the state of Wu consulted a shaman and found out what Luban had done. They sent him great gifts to appease him. Luban was kind and he could not bear the thought that his own individual wrath should cause such great suffering for innocent people. In the end, he cut down the hand of the wooden idol. Rain then fell upon the state of Wu.

The roofs of our country's temples and palaces are decorated with the heads and tails of dragons; door knockers are in the shape of carp. It is said that these designs had their origins with Luban. There is a myth among the people that Luban once borrowed a design for a dragon palace from the Sea Dragon King and promised to return it within three days. But after three days were up, he was not finished with it. So when the Sea Dragon King sent Little Sea Dragon leading a force of shrimp generals and carp soldiers to get the design back, Luban blocked the door to the Sea Dragon's palace after they had set out. When the army returned and could not get back inside, they were dried to death in the sun. So stricken, Little Sea Dragon lay on the top of the roof shingles and a carp was stuck to the door of ·the palace. After this, Luban followed this pattern in all his future building.

Luban made a 'wooden man cart' for his mother. This cart had a device which made the cart go very fast when rigged up. It was said that his mother was lost forever when she set out in the cart and never returned. In the Three King-doms Period, the cart invented by Chu Guo Gong Ming (the 'wooden cow, moving horse cart') was said to have followed closely the earlier example of Luban.

Luban also invented many woodworking tools such as the plane, the drill, the milling machine, the spade and the saw. It is said that the invention of the saw was inspired by his once having been cut by the serations on the edge of a blade of grass. Finding the many little teeth on the edges of the grass quite sharp, he applied the principle to the invention of the saw.

122

The Merchants' Association

The ink-line hook and workbench stop were also masterpieces of Luban's creation. Before these were invented, Luban's mother had to help him by holding the other end of the ink line so that he could mark the wood. He felt it a great inconvenience so he thought of adding a hook to the other end to take the place of his mother. Later, carpenters, in order to commemorate his filial invention, called the hook 'Luban's mother'.

When Luban planed wood, he always asked his wife to hold the wood for him to keep it from moving. Later he felt that since his wife had also to do the housework, serve his parents, and teach and care for their children, also having to assist him in his work was a great inconvenience and a waste of time. So he thought up a way of holding the wood in place by nailing a small piece of wood to the work bench, and later carpenters called this work bench stop 'Luban's wife'.

The calibrated ruler now used by carpenters is called Luban's ruler and is said to have been his invention.

Luban's wife was the equal of her husband in creative works. The umbrella we use on rainy days was her invention. So as a couple both Luban and his wife were quite outstanding.

The Merchants' Association hosts another entertainment meeting each year, and every two years at this meeting officers are elected, a formality in which any of the thirty-five positions below the Chairman, Vice-Chairman, Secretary and Treasurer are shuffled between as many members without much purpose.

The current Chairman has served for four consecutive two-year terms. He was raised in Hong Kong in pre-war days, of a family which made millions, reputedly by wangling a concession to unload garbage from warships entering colonial waters and converting the slop, by sale to New Territories farmers, into valuable animal feed and fertilizer. The Chairman knew the details of Hong Kong's pre-war economic infrastructure quite well, and proudly spoke the English of American sailors, with whom he had had much contact as a youth. In the late 1940s he invested a portion of his family fortune into art-carved furniture production, and the import–export business. He is one of the few art-carved furniture proprietors of his generation who never actually worked at either carving or carpentry. His familiarity with the Hong Kong scene is what made him an attractive candidate for the Chairmanship of the Merchants' Association. It is probable that the Honorary Advisory Board members of the Association were chosen upon his astute recommendation as to which personalities could be most helpful to the Association's interests. He is a fairly prominent Hong Kong personality and also holds responsible positions in his own surname association and in the powerful Tsimshatsui (tourist section) neighborhood association. As mentioned above, he is also a Lions Club member and sits on the board of the Tung Wah Hospital Group. There is probably no other Merchants' Association member with such extensive contacts. However, by 1973, the actual running of the family furniture business had passed onto his sons, and he was about to retire both as Association Chairman and from active business life. In recent years, little of his time has been devoted to Merchants' Association activity.

The other officers of the Merchants' Association are an Organization Officer, a Welfare Works Officer, a Communications Officer, an Entertainment Officer, a Propaganda Officer and the Vice- ————— Officer of all the above. There is an Advisory Board with members and reserve members, and a Supervisory Board with members and reserve members. The position of greatest importance, and no doubt entailing the most work among them all, is probably that of the Entertainment Officer. Most of the positions are of no account whatever, save providing labels for thirty-five contributing members at the yearly parties.

Thus, apart from occasional forays in response to threats to its members' interests, its regular yearly celebration on founder's day, etc., the Merchants' Association has not been active as an agent of change since shortly after 1964. The Association has not yet become an organization of big capitalists. It is still an organization of well-off family businessmen, whose days are numbered by the bigger firms, which are more able to absorb rising costs, and which have no interest in the Association. Most bosses are aware that the era of small capitalists is coming to a close in the Hong Kong art-carved furniture industry. Some have begun to expand their enterprises. Others place their hope in their sons to streamline and expand their enterprises with the abstract skills of modern business, rather than with the empirical skills of production technique upon which most of the senior generation of bosses relied. The furniture manufacturing industry is fast becoming one of big capital, but the Association at this stage has not adjusted itself to deal with changing conditions. At present, there is little the Association can provide for its family-firm members perched precariously between rising labor and production costs, all but static markets in their special commodity, and a price ceiling in competing and superior carved-furniture ware of Chinese Communist manufacture. The Association's Honorary Board Members in the higher echelons of government and business cannot be of much help in dealing with such problems either. The solution to such problems involves forces of greater magnitude than those at stake in the Whitfield squatters case.

Perhaps as the sons of Association members begin to become more active in expanding, further capitalizing and diversifying their production, the Association will revitalize and assume a more active role in promoting the interests of what will undoubtedly be a smaller group of bigger capitalists. Perhaps now that the current Chairman has all but stepped down, his replacement, the proprietor of one of the largest member firms, can with a fresh start begin this revitalization process.

For the moment, the Merchants' Association offers its members little beyond the security and dignity of knowing that, when they die, they will be interred in the proper traditional way.

8

Cheung Kung-ngai –
master carver *par excellence*

There are few carvers of Cheung Kung-ngai's ability in the Hong Kong art-carved furniture industry. The elaboration of the division of labor, the accumulation of capital, the introduction of machines, the further elaboration of the division of labor particularly in carpentry, diversification and growth in concentrations of capital have all contributed to the cheapening of the master carver's skills and to the undermining of his importance to the industry in which his skills once constituted the most important factor of marketability.

Nevertheless, several carvers, Cheung Kung-ngai among them, possessed of markedly superior carving skills, have to a considerable extent been able to sustain a less alienating relationship to their product, within less alienating relations of production, in which each product of their individual creation, whatever its ultimate fate – screen panel, coffee table top, restaurant or temple ornament – retains the character of a work of art in itself. This small group of highly skilled artisans, trained in pre-war China, may be seen today as fighting a rear-guard battle against the tendencies toward the cheapening of their skills in a more highly elaborated and highly capitalized division of labor, which began to develop with the onset of manufacture. Unfortunately, the larger campaign had already taken its decisive turn when the very first carver stepped beneath the roof of a coastal Shanghai furniture factory.

Like many of Hong Kong's better carvers, Cheung Kung-ngai is a Dongyang native. Now in his early sixties, he has been carving since he was twelve. He claims to have studied as a child with the most famous masters in Dongyang, and he has carved in Dongyang, Shanghai, Hangzhou and Ningbo. During the Japanese occupation he worked in the fields as a peasant laborer and, with the advent of the communist takeover of the Mainland, made his way to Hong Kong. In 1950 he returned to Zhejiang and got married, returning to Hong Kong shortly afterwards. His wife followed him out in 1958. He and his wife and five children now occupy a single room in a Hong Kong resettlement estate, which at the moment also serves as his workshop. He claims he makes enough to get 'two meals a day' (the Chinese equivalent of 'three square meals' as breakfast does

125

not count). I believe he does considerably better than that, but his prices are high and his sales may be infrequent.

The most exciting thing about Cheung's work is its genuine creativity. He despises the 'garbage' which passes for Chinese 'art' in the furniture stores of Canton Road. He does not restrict himself to the typical motifs which most carvers in the Hong Kong industry turn out in large quantities, but when he does execute them, they are of noticeably higher calibre. His skill is such that he is able to innovate beyond the bounds of this limited number of motifs, and he can reproduce animals, birds, insects of all shapes and species, plants of many different varieties and people in all walks of life. For him 'anything that can be seen in the world' is grist for his carving skill.

He possesses a large number of picture books from which inspiration for many of his works depicting mythical and historical characters and events come, but is also an avid student of nature and takes great pride in his ability to represent its diversity in wood (see Stanley 1914:78–9, on traditional Chinese design in wood). He lavishes great care on his pieces and one piece may take him as long as two or three months to complete. Every leaf of every plant in his carvings is given the most careful attention, and each figure, human or otherwise, is gracefully proportioned in exquisite detail.

While he is reputed to be one of the two most skillful carvers in all Hong Kong, Cheung belittles his own skill, in deference to those he believes to be the true masters still carving in Dongyang, Zhejiang, and he declines the title *huang-di* emperor (see Chapter 3).

Cheung prefers to be his own boss, although he has worked in factories in the past, and may very well be forced to do so again in the future. It is only possible for him to maintain his status as an independent craftsman because of the high quality and uniqueness of his carvings, which he sells, as the market will bear, on a piece-by-piece basis to furniture factories, retailers, restaurants, temples and individuals in Hong Kong and Taiwan. As the cost of maintaining a worker in Hong Kong continues to rise, the relatively enormous portion of labor time which goes into his creations, and their consequent high price, may make his sales less and less frequent, and he may be forced to re-enter the assembly line as a wage earner to maintain his 'two meals a day'. He has done so from time to time in the past when orders for his high-priced special-order pieces declined in number. Nevertheless, when I revisited Cheung in 1978, he had sufficient advance orders to keep him working for a year or two.

His frame of mind is not proletarian, and Cheung refuses to let it become so. The relations of production which characterize his enterprise are rather like those of the independent rural temple carvers who, in the early years of the art-carved furniture industry, produced independent pieces of temple ornamentation in their homes to be built into newly constructed furniture on the coast. He sees each piece of work as his own and, as the artist, expects the recognition and profit due him for his labor. His product is the end result of the labor of his hands alone, despite the fact that, as in the Shanghai-based industry of the Republican period, many of his 'finished' creations are destined for inclusion in camphorwood chests, screens or coffee tables — items of furniture for export to Europeans. He remains, in a sense, on the industry's fringes.

Cheung has no patience with the proletarian discourse of the Woodwork Carvers' Union and, while he does not think a great deal of Chiang Kai-shek, professes a strong hatred of 'communism'. He recognizes that drug addiction, crime, corruption and prostitution are evils inherent in a free enterprise system, but prefers the 'freedom' of Hong Kong to life under communism. He is a great advocate of 'democracy' and admires the United States although he has never been there. Yet, along with many Chinese of varying political persuasions in Hong Kong, Cheung believes that there is probably 'too much freedom' in the United States.

Despite the negative feelings he expressed toward communism in 1973, Cheung returned to China, for the first time since the 1950s, in 1975 and again in 1976, for a month each time, to visit his native village in Dongyang county. While there, several friends and relations tried to convince him to remain and carve in Zhejiang where he would have a house and fields. While noting that in Zhejiang he would have been able to retire at sixty, whereas in Hong Kong he will have to work till he drops, he nevertheless declined the offer, preferring Hong Kong where he can buy what he wants, drink when he wants, gamble when he wants, etc. However, he prefers the present Hua/Deng regime to past Chinese governments.

Cheung's relations with the Woodwork Carvers' Union have never been good and, although he claims to have been a member in the 1950s, he was considered a troublemaker in those quarters. He assured me that, had I arrived on the scene five years earlier, prior to the *détente* between the United States and China which began in earnest during my stay in Hong Kong, I would have been immediately characterized as a spy, and more than likely railroaded out of the industry at that time by the communist union; an appraisal probably pretty close to the mark.

Cheung is encouraged in his feelings about the evils of communism, among other reasons, by his ready access to a black market in carvings made for private gain in Communist China by carvers employed in the production of furniture for export there. Somehow, small carvings produced in rural Zhejiang towns are sold privately in Shanghai and smuggled out to Hong Kong for sale without the knowledge of the authorities. Cheung obtains these carvings from time to time and sells them at a sizeable profit where he can, 'to help his fellow carvers get by under the rigors of communism'. To what extent these carvers need the extra money simply 'to get by' remains to be determined. That such practices exist, there is little doubt. I have seen the carvings involved and they are quite beautiful, far surpassing the level of craftsmanship which dominates the Hong Kong industry.

The wood-carvers of Hong Kong

As to the future of his profession in Hong Kong, where speed and quantity rather than quality, originality, versatility and expressiveness are at a premium, Cheung is not optimistic. While he has taken on apprentices in the past, and while I cannot imagine a better master from whom to learn the skills of carving, Cheung will not teach his skills to his son. He realizes that carving skills offer no means of gaining a livelihood outside the art-carved furniture industry in Hong Kong, and that the future of the art-carved furniture industry itself is far from secure. He would agree with most of his colleagues who feel their craft is 'useless' and that there is no future in it. While Cheung maintains a more secure pride in his skills than do many of his fellow carvers, he has no illusions about the potential earning power of a carver.

With no regrets at having spent his own life as a carver, he wants a better life for his son, and would rather see him go into business than have anything to do with carving. Cheung is well aware that the rear-guard action, in which he and a few others like him are engaged, cannot stem the tide which threatens the very existence of their profession.

9

Summary and conclusions

By now it should be clear that the concept of manufacture provides a powerful analytical model which at once explains, as it is exemplified in, the evolution of the Chinese art-carved furniture industry. It provides a perspective from which to analyze how the all-leveling rationality of the capitalist mode of production became manifest in the course of the evolution of craft production, and provides a useful watershed in which to isolate the key social, economic and political transformations in the relations of craft production that characterize that evolution.

To summarize briefly: under a regime of manufacture, the labor power of skilled artisans was arrayed in a unified and systematized division of labor that allowed maximum productivity in a technological regime of hand power. A competitive unit of carved-furniture production required a staff of roughly 30 workers in proportions of roughly 16 carvers (8 rough: 8 smooth): 12 carpenters: 2 painters. Skilled craft workers retained ownership of a significant portion of the means of production, although the productive power which resulted from their combined efforts allowed the organizer of that productive power, the capitalist, to accumulate capital steadily, and to a greater extent than ever before. Income differences between boss and worker widened gradually and prepared the way for a shift in concentration of ownership of the means of production almost entirely into capitalist hands when it became possible to introduce power-driven machines into the division of labor. This latter event announced the end of hand manufacture.

As workers grew progressively more alienated from the means of production, and finally became almost totally so, whatever remnants of traditional protectionist privileges enjoyed by the workers that had survived into the period of manufacture, came to be more and more a matter of cash loans than favors in kind. Day labor became more prominent as a measure of remuneration than piecework.

A commercial structure founded on association by same native place yielded to an industry-wide association of petty traders as the manufacturing regime was eclipsed. The commercial structure had become cemented together by larger firms which did business with all comers. Such principles of business operation became dominant and later even superseded the organizational scope of the petty traders' association.

Craft parochialism, which characterized the traditional economic setting, was still present in several forms, both in business relations and in the art-carved furniture labor force throughout the period of manufacture. Yet the social underpinnings of discrete groups of separate craftsmen, in different woods, of differing native places, were challenged in this period by more universalistic political forces which, while not yet dominant in the social divisions of the manufacturing workforce, later came to be so, as the material conditions of production in the industry came to reflect an increasing polarization of classes and class interest.

This challenge was represented in the activities of the Woodwork Carvers' Union which were quite noteworthy in three respects.

First, the union acted as a synthesizer of a variety of elements in the social and ideological superstructure of craft production in Hong Kong, whose origins and functions derived from both pre-capitalist and capitalist modes of production. In this context, the union played a significant role in recombining, redefining and giving new content to the distinctive functions of the pre-capitalist elements as they became increasingly subordinated to the demands of the emerging dominant capitalist mode.

Secondly, the union served as the agent by means of which an ideology informed by a proletarian consciousness, incorporating those elements corresponding to the capitalist mode, gradually emerged as dominant.

Finally, the union's activity in both the above respects provides a concrete illustration of the analytical usefulness of Godelier's delimitation of the scope of the concepts of mode of production and social formation. For Godelier, analysis of the ways in which the distinctive functions of superstructural elements which originate in different modes of production are combined, redefined and given new content as one mode of production subjects the others to its dominance, constitutes the final step in producing 'a synthetic definition of the precise nature of the diversity and unity of the economic and social relations which characterize a society at a given epoch' (Godelier 1974:1).

The specific recombinations and redefinitions to which such superstructural elements are subject are ultimately dependent on the specific resources that the various emergent classes are capable of mustering in their own cause. While highly skilled labor, indispensable and intractable, at first had the upper hand in the art-carved furniture industry, its unity was seriously disrupted by parochial tendencies inherited from a guild-dominated past.

The introduction of power-driven machines marked the upper limit in the disproportionate growth of the power of capital under a regime of manufacture, and ushered in a new regime with a whole series of new technical requirements and possibilities. These to a great extent determined the future course of the development of the art-carved furniture industry by making diversification into modern, less elaborately carved furniture an attractive strategy, by further undermining the skills of the handcraftsmen of the manufacturing division of labor, and by lending an even more proletarian character to the labor force and boss—worker relations.

But the introduction of machines marked only a climax over and above the considerable amount of groundwork in the process of class polarization and proletarianization which had already been laid in rearrangements in the relations of production under hand manufacture. The progressively increasing portion of the proceeds of production which came to accrue to capital during this period, created the basis for the introduction of expensive power-driven machines. The unity of the production process itself had already become the property of capital, and capital a ruling power over labor.

It is this emergence of the bosses as a permanent capitalist class that is the most significant development in hand manufacture, although this development was accompanied in the art-carved furniture industry by a corresponding growing proletarian militance on the part of highly skilled labor, whose skills were increasingly compromised. Armed with an ever more appropriate 'working class' ideology, organized labor struggled to maintain the preponderance and exclusive character of skilled labor and the high wages which go with it, recombining and redefining the content of traditional elements of the superstructure of craft production, making them serve new purposes. Apprenticeship, as the institution-alized means of labor force reproduction, constitutes one important focus of this struggle between labor and the emergent capitalist class.

Hindess and Hirst, in a discussion of transitional modes of production, have argued that 'The possibility or otherwise of transition depends upon the specific forms of class struggle, its concrete objectives and the forces that can be mobilized in support of these objectives' (1975:280).

Similarly, Marglin, in a recent article, has emphasized the importance of the relative power positions of emergent and competing classes in determining the course of social and technological change, and has argued that the analysis of such phenomena 'require[s] models that are grounded in the challenge—response mechanism of class conflict, models at once dynamic and dialectic' (1974:108).

The concept of manufacture provides an analytical basis for the construction of such models, highlighting as it does the emergence of an increasingly bipolar class structure from a pre-existing cluster of discrete socio-economic groups, and the processes by which these emergent classes mobilize the resources to struggle in their increasingly divided interests.

The institutional configuration which characterizes manufacture may vary from industry to industry in a given social formation with the specific material conditions of the industry; with the existence of sufficient demand to stimulate and/or absorb the increased productivity which manufacture allows (see

Georgescu-Roegen 1971:249); with the nature of the product; with the availability of labor and the level of its requisite skill or skills; with the degree to which an industry is subject to excessive state or bureaucratic exactions or to international competition from machine-produced substitutes or superior-quality lines. Such factors will all affect the respective power positions of the emergent classes, and therefore also affect the way in which decisions influencing the course of the development of the industry in question will be made, ultimately determining the possibility or otherwise of transition to industrial capitalism.

Kahn (1975:146–7) has described the development of simple commodity production in Western Sumatra, where a number of structural constraints arising out of the relation of the simple commodity mode to a traditional subsistence sector, and to the world capitalist system, create a cyclical movement of the forces of production quite different from the cumulative movement described in this study. A kind of negative feedback mechanism involving rewards for labor, the local price of rice, and a price ceiling established by competing products of western manufacture conduces to inhibit technological innovation and an advance to full-scale industrial capitalism.

Certain Chinese crafts remained frozen in a regime of manufacture for several hundred years before the arrival of the western capitalist powers on China's shores. Herman quotes an authority on the production of Qing dynasty porcelain at Jing De Zhen who describes a division of labor clearly characteristic of manufacture:

Division of labor prevailed to an extent scarcely outdone by the most modern industrial organizations. Throwing, moulding, assembling of parts, painting of the various subjects, each was the concern of separate workmen. The outlines of the blue painted decoration were drawn by one hand, to be filled by washes by another . . . A piece would sometimes pass through as many as seventy hands (Herman 1954:127).

Porcelain 'manufacture' can therefore be spoken of as dating back some 300 years in Chinese history. Why no permanent capitalist class emerged from such institutional arrangements, or why such arrangements never ended in an industrial revolution in China prior to contact with the west, has yet to be satisfactorily explained (Elvin 1972 provides some interesting hypotheses), and remains a source of considerable debate. For our present purposes, it only bears repeating that in the course of history 'the division of labor peculiar to manufacture acquires the best adapted form at first by experience . . . and here and there succeeds in keeping it for centuries' (Marx 1967:1:364).

The existence, as a rational option of investment, of newly won profits in technological innovation by an emergent capitalist class clearly does not follow inevitably from the institutional structure of manufacture itself. What then is the significance of the discovery of manufacture in Hong Kong?

Summary and conclusions

Samir Amin has argued that 'the pattern of transition to peripheral capitalism is fundamentally different from that of transition to central capitalism' (Amin 1976:200; see also Frank 1967; Roseberry 1976; Wallerstein 1974). 'The onslaught from without by means of trade carried out by the capitalist mode of production upon pre-capitalist formations causes certain crucial retrogressions to take place such as the ruin of crafts without their being replaced by local industrial production' (Amin 1976:200).

There is certainly evidence of such retrogression in the imperialist experience of China. Feuerwerker has shown, for example, how, in the spinning and weaving of cotton cloth in nineteenth and twentieth century China, 'handicraft workshops appeared in substantial numbers only after modern industries had been brought forth directly or indirectly by foreign investment, and then only as ancillaries to the mechanized factories' (Feuerwerker 1969:29).

A middle period of transition, of primitive accumulation, in which a peasant side-occupation could evolve through a regime of manufacture was precluded. A manufacturing division of labor did not constitute a competitive alternative to production which had already undergone a revolution in the instruments of labor. The transition to capitalism in such cases was clearly of a different nature from that of central capitalist countries.*

While Hong Kong clearly displays the disarticulation of economy that Amin finds characteristic of social formations in the periphery of the world capitalist system, it is precisely this disarticulated character which makes it possible, *at the level of the mode of production*, to discover sectors whose development clearly manifests the well-established patterns of the evolution of the capitalist mode of production described by Marx for sixteenth–eighteenth-century Europe (see Chapter 1), in which the pattern of transition to peripheral capitalism does not differ substantially from that of transition to central capitalism.

The Hong Kong based art-carved furniture industry provides a very concrete example of this pattern. Shielded as it was from international competition by the nature of its products' marketable features (elaborate carving) and the post Korean War trade embargo, on the products of its only competitor (the Peoples' Republic of China), it evolved institutions of primitive accumulation virtually identical to those which Marx described for Europe. Amin himself has noted with respect to the development of the simple commodity mode of production that 'the less this mode of production is hindered by other modes, the more striking will be the capitalist development it engenders' (Amin 1974a: 379).

---

* Just how extensive the debilitating effects of the western imperialist 'onslaught from without' were to the economy of nineteenth- and twentieth-century China, as a whole, is a widely debated point (see Esherick's exchange with Nathan, *Bulletin of Concerned Asian Scholars*, 1972:4:4:3–16; see Potter 1968:174ff for a good summary of the arguments on both sides; see also Myers 1970), and one which I can scarcely resolve in the context of the present study.

The wood-carvers of Hong Kong

The example of the art-carved furniture industry makes it possible to elaborate further on the ideas of Amin regarding the structure of the peripheral formations of the world capitalist system. It suggests that peripheral formations themselves are possessed of an internal structure of center and periphery which for the sake of terminological clarity I shall call core and margin. Industries at the *core* of peripheral formations manifest greater dependence on the world capitalist center; those at the *margin* of peripheral formations manifest less dependence – a kind of negation of a negation if I may be permitted a dialectical indulgence. Whereas capitalist development becomes deformed at the core of peripheral formations, at the margin, certain sectors may enjoy the luxury of a relatively *laissez-faire*, albeit still export-oriented, capitalist development.

While not drawing out the core–margin structure of peripheral formations, Amin has noted that competition with foreign capital necessarily drives the national bourgeoisie of the capitalist periphery into complementary sectors 'that have been left to it' (1974a:162), and goes on to describe these sectors as a 'margin' in which a certain amount of accumulation for the benefit of a national bourgeoisie can occur (1974a:382).

Amin has further argued that the tendency present in formations of the world capitalist center for the capitalist mode of production to become exclusive, based on a widening and deepening of its internal market, is not present in peripheral formations (1974b:72), or at best occurs 'only to the extent allowed by an "international specialization" in which the periphery remains passive . . . ' (1974a:177).

The experience of the art-carved furniture industry provides an opportunity to hypothesize that where international specialization makes possible the spread of the capitalist mode of production, that is, at the margins of peripheral social formations, a tendency for the capitalist mode to become exclusive may be observed based on a widening and deepening of the *external market* at well.

It is significant that Marx has noted with respect to Europe that:

The original historic forms in which capital appears, at first sporadically or *locally*, alongside the old modes of production, while exploding them little by little everywhere, is . . . manufacture proper (not yet the factory); this springs up where mass quantities are produced for export, for the external market – i.e. on the *basis of large-scale overland and maritime commerce* . . . where production is thus, so to speak *naturally* oriented towards exchange value (Marx 1939: 510–11, emphasis in the original).

Whereas Amin has argued that in peripheral formations the dominant capitalist mode of production subdues and transforms the others, disfiguring them, depriving them of their functionality and subjecting them to its own, he maintains that these subordinate modes are not radically disintegrated and destroyed (Amin 1974b:72), but are rather rendered dependent on the capitalist center.

The findings of this study make it possible to conclude, however, that, as

134

Summary and conclusions

the coexisting modes on the margins of the capitalist periphery are subdued and transformed, as they are deprived of their functionality, as they are subjected to the all-leveling rationality of the capitalist mode of production, these subordinate modes, rather than continuing to exist in disfigured or distorted form, *may indeed be radically made over in the very image of the capitalist mode of production.*

It is tempting to suggest that, in the course of time, such sectors in the margin of the periphery may develop to the point at which their position in the structure of the periphery converges with that of core sectors. When art-carved furniture manufacturers turned to the production of contemporary furniture, it might be argued that they effectively assumed a position squarely in the core of the Hong Kong peripheral formation, where they became exposed to outright competition with products of the Eruopean capitalist center. One crucial difference, however, is apparent insofar as the consolidation of a regime of primitive accumulation in a period of manufacture in the post-war period allowed carved-furniture producers successfully to launch an internationally competitive, capitalistically organized modern furniture industry from a position of relative strength. The level of dependence on the world capitalist center of emergent capitalism in the margin of the periphery remains quite restricted and is manifest only in a continuing export-oriented reliance on the international market.

Thus, as well as providing the analytical wherewithal to make the present-day transition from craft to industry intelliglble, the discovery of manufacture in Hong Kong also provides the basis for further hypotheses regarding the structure and evolution of social formations of the periphery of the world capitalist system.

Hopefully, this study has provided an example of how Marxist concepts may be usefully employed in contemporary anthropological practice. If it has made the reader increasingly sceptical of facile dismissals of Marxist analyses and concepts as irrelevant to the analysis of contemporary socio-economic phenomena, and contributed in a small way to the growing legitimacy of Marxist analysis in western social science, I would deem it to have been a success.

BIBLIOGRAPHY

Abegglen, J. (1958). *The Japanese Factory*. Glencoe:Free Press.

Abend, Hallet (1944). *Treaty Ports*. New York:Doubleday.

Agarwala, A.N. (1963). *The Economics of Underdevelopment*. New York: Oxford University Press.

Althusser, Louis (1970). *For Marx*. New York:Vintage.

Amin, S. (1974a). *Accumulation on a World Scale*. New York:Monthly Review Press.

— (1974b). 'Modes of Production and Social Formations', *Ufahamu*, 4:57–85.

— (1976). *Unequal Development*. New York:Monthly Review Press.

Arnold, Julean H. (1922). *Changes in the Economic Life of the Chinese People*. Washington, D.C.:Government Printing Office.

— (1930). 'Modern Industry in China', *Chinese Economic Journal* (hereafter *CEJ*), 7:1066.

Asad, T. and Wolpe, H. (1976). 'Concepts of Modes of Production', *Economy and Society*, 5:470.

Association for Radical East Asian Studies (1970). 'Hong Kong:Britain's Last Colonial Stronghold', Mimeo.

Avineri, Shlomo (ed.) (1969). *Karl Marx on Colonialism and Modernization*. Garden City:Anchor.

Baker, Hugh (1968). *Sheung Shui: A Chinese Lineage Village*. London:Cass.

Baran, Paul (1957). *The Political Economy of Growth*. New York:Monthly Review Press.

Baran, Paul and Hobsbawm, E. (1970). 'The Stages of Economic Growth', in Mermelstein (ed.) *Economics: Mainstream Readings and Radical Critiques*.

Baran, Paul and Sweezey, Paul (1966). *Monopoly Capital*. New York:Monthly Review Press.

Bauer, P. T. and Yamey, B. (1957). *Economics of Underdeveloped Countries*. Cambridge:Cambridge University Press

Belshaw, C. (1965). *Traditional Exchange and Modern Markets*. Englewood Cliffs:Prentice-Hall.

Benham, F. C. (1956). 'The Growth of Manufacturing in Hong Kong', *International Affairs*, 32(4):456.

Bloch, M. (ed.) (1975). *Marxist Analyses and Social Anthropology*. London: Malaby Press.

Bibliography

Bottomley, A. (1965). 'The Fate of the Artisan in Developing Economies', *Social and Economic Studies*, 14:194.

Brackett, Oliver (1924). *The Life of Chippendale*. London:Hodder & Stoughton, Ltd.

Braverman, Harry (1974). *Labor and Monopoly Capital*. New York:Monthly Review Press.

Bücher, Karl (1901). *Industrial Evolution*. New York:Wicket, Holt & Co.

Burgess, J. S. (1928). *The Guilds of Peking*. New York:Columbia University Press.

Cairncross, A. (1964). 'The Place of Capital in Economic Progress' in Gerald Meier (ed.), *Leading Issues in Development Economics*. New York:Oxford University Press.

Campbell, D. (1965).'Variation and Selective Retention in Socio-cultural Evolution' in Barringer *et al.* (eds.), *Social Change in Developing Areas*. Cambridge:Schenkman.

Cancian, F. (1966). 'Modernization Theories and the Study of Economic Development', *American Anthropologist*, 62:802.

Carew, Tim. (1960). *The Fall of Hong Kong*. London:Pan Books.

Castenada, Carlos (1968). *The Teachings of Don Juan*. New York:Simon & Schuster.

– (1971). *A Separate Reality*. New York:Simon & Schuster.

– (1972). *Journey to Ixtlan*. New York:Simon & Schuster.

– (1976). *Tales of Power*. New York:Simon & Schuster.

Census and Statistics Department (Hong Kong Government) (1972a). *Hong Kong Population and Housing Census 1971*. Hong Kong:Government Printer.

– (1972b). *Monthly Digest of Statistics*, June. Hong Kong:Government Printer.

– (1972c). *The 1971 Census: A Graphic Guide*. Hong Kong:Government Printer.

– (1973). *Hong Kong Review of Overseas Trade in 1972*. Hong Kong:Government Printer.

Chang, John K. (1969). *Industrial Development in Pre-Communist China*. Edinburgh:Edinburgh University Press.

Ch'en, Ta (1927a). *Analysis of Strikes in China from 1918–1926*. Shanghai: Chinese Bureau of Economic Information.

– (1927b). *The Labor Movement in China*. Peking: Peking Leader Press.

Cheng, Ngai-lung (1976). 'Underdevelopment and the World Capitalist System', unpublished M.Sc. thesis, University of Salford, England.

Chesneaux, Jean (1968). *The Chinese Labor Movement 1919–1929*. Stanford: Stanford University Press.

Childe, V. G. (1950). 'The Urban Revolution'. *Town Planning Review* 21.

Chinese Economic Journal (the editors of) (1927a). 'Labor Conditions in Chekiang, 1:216.

– (1927b). 'Strikes in Shanghai in 1926', 1:227.

– (1928). 'Shanghai Match Factories', 3:865.

– (1932a). 'The Glass Industry in China', 10:426.

– (1932b). 'The Match Industry in China', 10:197.

– (1932c). 'The Soap Industry in China', 10:113.

– (1932d). 'The Straw Hat Industry in China', 10:141.

Bibliography

- (1932e). 'Umbrella Manufacture in China', 11:63.
Chippendale, Thomas (1754). *The Gentleman and Cabinet Maker's Directory*. London:the author.
Ch'u, C. C. and Blaisdell, T. C. (1924). 'Peking Rugs and Peking Boys', *Chinese Social and Political Review*, Special Supplement.
Cole, Robert (1971). *Japanese Blue Collar*. Berkeley:University of California Press.
Commissioner of Labor, Hong Kong (1951–2). *Annual Report*. Hong Kong: Government Printer.
- (1960–1). *Annual Report*. Hong Kong:Government Printer.
- (1964–5). *Annual Report*. Hong Kong:Government Printer.
Cook, Scott (1966a). 'Our Obsolete "Anti-Market" Mentality', *American Anthropologist*, 68:323.
- (1966b). 'Maximization, Economic Theory and Anthropology', *American Anthropologist*, 68:1494.
Cooper, Eugene (1973). 'An Interview with China's Anthropologists', *Current Anthropology*, 14:4.
Cooper, John (1970). *Colony in Conflict*. Hong Kong:Swindon Book Co.
Crissman, Lawrence (1967). 'The Segmentary Structure of Urban Overseas Chinese Communities', *Man* 2:185.
- (1972). 'Marketing on the Chang Hua Plain, Taiwan', in W. E. Wilmott (ed.), *Economic Organization in Chinese Society*.
Crossman, C. L. (1972). *The China Trade*. Princeton:Pyne Press.
Dalton, George (1960). 'A Note of Clarification on Economic Surplus', *American Anthropologist*, 62:483.
- (1961). 'Economic Theory and Primitive Society', *American Anthropologist*, 63:1.
- (1963). 'Economic Surplus: Once Again', *American Anthropologist*, 65:389.
- (1967). 'Bibliographical Essay', in G. Dalton (ed.), *Tribal and Peasant Economies*. New York:Natural History Press.
- (1968). 'Economics, Economic Development and Economic Anthropology', *Journal of Economic Issues*, 2:173.
- (1969a). 'Economics, Anthropology, and Economic Anthropology', in O. Von Mering (ed.), *Anthropology and Related Disciplines*.
- (1969b). 'Issues in Economic Anthropology', *Current Anthropology*, 10:63.
Davis, S. G. (1949). *Hong Kong in its Geographical Setting*. London:Collins.
De Glopper, Donald R. (1969). 'The Taoist Ethic and the Spirit of Petty Capitalism in the Business Relations of Lukang Taiwan', unpublished paper prepared for the research conference on Economic Organization in Chinese Society, St Adele en haut, Quebec.
- (1972). 'Doing Business in Lukang', in W. E. Wilmott (ed.), *Economic Organization in Chinese Society*.
Department of Industry and Commerce (Hong Kong Government) (1946–7). *Annual Report*. Hong Kong:Government Printer.
- (1947–8). *Annual Report*. Hong Kong:Government Printer.
- (1948–9). *Annual Report*. Hong Kong:Government Printer.
- (1949–50). *Annual Report*. Hong Kong:Government Printer.
- (1950–1). *Annual Report*. Hong Kong:Government Printer.
- (1951–2). *Annual Report*. Hong Kong:Government Printer.
-

Bibliography

- (1952–3). *Annual Report.* Hong Kong:Government Printer.
- (1953–4). *Annual Report.* Hong Kong:Government Printer.

Directory and Chronicle of China, Japan, Straits Settlements, and Malaya.
    (1913). Hong Kong:Hong Kong Daily Press.
- (1923). Hong Kong:Hong Kong Daily Press.
- (1940). Hong Kong:Hong Kong Daily Press.

District Commissioner New Territories (Hong Kong Government) (1952–3).
    Annual Report. Hong Kong:Government Printer.
- (1953–4). *Annual Report.* Hong Kong:Government Printer.
- (1954–5). *Annual Report.* Hong Kong:Government Printer.
- (1955–6). *Annual Report.* Hong Kong:Government Printer.
- (1956–7). *Annual Report.* Hong Kong:Government Printer.
- (1957–8). *Annual Report.* Hong Kong:Government Printer.

Dobb, Maurice (1947). *Studies in the Development of Capitalism.* London: Routledge.

Donald, Leland (1974). Review of D. Hymes (ed.). *Reinventing Anthropology, American Anthropologist,* 76:857.

Dupre, Georges and Rey, Pierre-Phillipe (1978). 'Reflections on the Relevance of a Theory of the History of Exchange', in D. Seddon (ed.), *Relations of Production: Marxist Approaches to Economic Anthropology.* London: Cass.

Dwyer, D. J. (1971). *Asian Urbanization: A Hong Kong Casebook.* Hong Kong: Hong Kong University Press.

Dwyer, D. J. and Lai, T. C. (1967). *The Small Industrial Unit in Hong Kong: Patterns and Policies.* London:Hull.

Ecke, Gustav (1944). *Chinese Domestic Furniture.* Peking:Henri Vetch.

Eddy, Elizabeth (1968). *Urban Anthropology: Research Perspectives and Strategies.* Athens: University of Georgia Press.

Elliot, Elsie (1971). *The Avarice, Bureaucracy and Corruption of Hong Kong.* Hong Kong:Friends Commercial Printing.

Elvin, Mark (1972). 'The High Level Equilibrium Trap', in W. E. Wilmott (ed.), *Economic Organization in Chinese Society.*
- (1973). *The Pattern of the Chinese Past.* Stanford: Stanford University Press.

Engels, Frederick (1959). 'History of the Communist League', in L. Feuer (ed.), *Marx and Engels.* Garden City:Anchor.

England, Joe (1971). 'Industrial Relations in Hong Kong', in K. Hopkins (ed.), *Hong Kong: The Industrial Colony.*

Esherick, Joseph (1972). 'Harvard on China: The Apologetics of Imperialism', *Bulletin of Concerned Asian Scholars,* 4:9.

Fairbank, J. K. *et al.* (1965). *East Asia, The Modern Transformation.* Boston: Houghton, Mifflin Co.

Fan, Pai-ch'uan (1962). 'The Condition and Fate of Chinese Handicrafts after the Penetration of Foreign Capitalism'. Peking:Li Shih Yen Chiu.

Fang, Fu-an (1930). 'Shanghai Labor', *CEJ,* 7:853, 989.
- (1931). *Chinese Labor.* Shanghai:Kelley & Walsh.

Far Eastern Economic Review, editors of (1967). Hong Kong Columns, May 18–December 21.

Fei, Hsiao-t'ung (1939). *Peasant Life in China.* London:Routledge.

Ferguson, John C. (1939). *Survey of Chinese Art.* Shanghai: Commercial Press.

Feuerwerker, Albert (1958). *China's Early Modernization.* New York:Atheneum.

Bibliography

- (1968). *The Chinese Economy, 1912–1949.* Michigan Papers in Chinese Studies No. 1.
- (1969). *The Chinese Economy, 1870–1911.* Michigan Papers in Chinese Studies No. 5.

First International Conference of Economic History (1960). Stockholm, Paris: Mouton.

Firth, R. (ed.) (1967). *Themes in Economic Anthropology*, A.S.A. Monograph No. 6. London:Tavistock.

Fong, H. D. (1929). *Tientsin Carpet Industry*, Nankai Institute of Economics Industry Series No. 1. Tientsin:Chihli Press.
- (1930a). *Rayon and Cotton Weaving in Tientsin*, Nankai Institute of Economics Industry Series No. 2. Tientsin:Chihli Press.
- (1930b). *Hosiery Knitting in Tientsin*, Nankai Institute of Economics Industry Series No. 3. Tientsin:Chihli Press.
- (1931). *China's Industrialization: A Statistical Survey*, Institute of Pacific Relations Conference Paper. Hangchow.
- (1934). *Grain Trade and Milling in Tientsin*, Nankai Institute of Economics Industry Series No. 6. Tientsin:Chihli Press.
- (1935). *Rural Weaving and the Merchant Employers in a North China District*, Nankai Institute of Economics Industry Series No. 7. Tientsin: Chihli Press.
- (1936). *Industrial Capital in China*, Nankai Institute of Economics Industry Series No. 9. Tientsin:Chihli Press.
- (1937). *Industrial Organization in China.* Nankai Institute of Economics Industry Series No. 10. Tientsin:Chihli Press.

Fong, H. D. and Ku, Y. T. (1934–5). 'Shoemaking in a North China Port', *Chinese Social and Political Science Review*, 18:505.

Foster-Carter, Aidan (1978). 'The Modes of Production Controversy', *New Left Review*, 107:47.

Frank, A. G. (1967). 'The Sociology of Underdevelopment and the Underdevelopment of Sociology', *Catalyst*, 3:20.

Freedman, M. (1958). *Lineage Organization in Southeastern China.* London: Athlone.

Fried, Morton H. (1953). *The Fabric of Chinese Society.* New York:Praeger.

Friedman, Jonathan (1972). 'System, Structure and Contradiction in the Evolution of Asiatic Social Formations'. Unpublished Ph.D. manuscript Columbia University. Ann Arbor:University Microfilms.

Gamble, Sidney D. (1921). *Peking: A Social Survey.* New York:George A. Doron Co.

Geertz, Clifford (1963a). *Pedlars and Princes.* Chicago: University of Chicago Press.
- (1963b). *Agricultural Involution.* Berkeley:University of California Press.

Georgescu-Roegen, Nicholas (1971). *The Entropy Law and the Economic Process.* Cambridge: Harvard University Press.

Godelier, Maurice (1972). *Rationality and Irrationality in Economics.* New York:Monthly Review Press.
- (1974). 'On the Definition of a Social Formation', *Critique of Anthropology*, 1:63.
- (1977). *Perspectives in Marxist Anthropology*, Cambridge Studies in Social Anthropology No. 18. Cambridge:Cambridge University Press.

Bibliography

Goode, William J. (1963). 'Industrialization and Family Change', in Hoselitz and Moore (eds.), *Industrialization and Society*.

Haberler, G. (1964). 'Critical Observations on Some Current Notions in the Theory of Economic Development', in Novack and Lekachman (eds.), *Development and Society*. New York:St Martin's Press.

Hammond, J. C. and B. (1947). *The Rise of Modern Industry*. London:Methuen.

Harris, Marvin (1959). 'The Economy has no Surplus?', *American Anthropologist*, 61:185.

– (1968). *The Rise of Anthropological Theory*. New York:Crowell.

Hauser, Phillip (1963). 'The Social, Economic and Technological Problems of Rapid Urbanization', in Hoselitz and Moore (eds.), *Industrialization and Society*.

Herman, Theodore (1954). 'An Analysis of China's Export Handicrafts Industries to 1930', unpublished Ph.D. manuscript. Ann Arbor:University Microfilms.

– (1955–6). 'The Role of Cottage and Small Scale Industries in Asian Economic Development', *Economic Development and Cultural Change*, 4:356.

– (1956–7). 'Cottage Industries: A Reply', *Economic Development and Cultural Change*, 5:374.

Hinder, Eleanor (1944). *Life and Labour in Shanghai*. New York: Institute of Pacific Relations.

Hindess, Barry and Hirst, Paul (1975). *Pre-Capitalist Modes of Production*. London:Routledge & Kegan Paul.

– (1977). *Modes of Production and Social Formations*. London:Macmillan Press.

Hirschman, Albert (1964). 'Population Pressure as a Force for Economic Development', in Novack and Lekachman (eds.), *Development and Society*.

Ho, Franklin and Fong, H. D. (1929). Extent and Effects of Industrialization in China. Nankai University Committee on Social and Economic Research, Tientsin.

Ho, P. Y. (ed.) (1935). *China Industrial Handbook*, Chekiang, Shanghai Bureau of Foreign Trade.

Hobsbawm, E. J. (1968). *Industry and Empire*. Harmondsworth:Penguin.

Hommel, Rudolf P. (1937). *China at Work*. New York:M.I.T. Press (1969).

Hong Kong Album (1960). *Hong Kong Album*. Hong Kong:South China Morning Post.

– (1961). *Hong Kong Album*. Hong Kong:South China Morning Post.

Hong Kong and Kowloon Art-Carved Furniture and Camphorwood Chests Merchants' Association (1963). *Art-Carved Furniture and Camphorwood Chests made in Hong Kong*. Hong Kong:Special Issue.

Hong Kong Directory (1961). *Hong Kong Directory*. Hong Kong:Government Printer.

– (1973). *Hong Kong Directory*. Hong Kong:Government Printer.

Hong Kong Federation of Trade Unions (1972–3). *Hong Kong Worker* (*Heung Kong Kuna Yan*). Hong Kong: Hong Kong Federation of Trade Unions.

Hong Kong Government Press (1965). *A Hong Kong Bibliography*. Hong Kong: Hong Kong Government Press.

– (1972). *Hong Kong 1971*. Hong Kong: Hong Kong Government Press.

– (1973). *Hong Kong 1973: A Review of 1972*. Hong Kong: Hong Kong Government Press.

Bibliography

Hong Kong Productivity Council (1972). 'Statistics on the Furniture Industry in Hong Kong', Mimeo.
Hong Kong Research Project (1974). *Hong Kong: A Case to Answer*. Nottingham:Russell Press.
Hong Kong Trade Statistics (1972). *Exports and Reexports (December)*. Hong Kong:Government Printer.
  – (1973). *Exports and Reexports (December)*. Hong Kong:Government Printer.
  – (1974). *Exports and Reexports (December)*. Hong Kong:Government Printer.
  – (1975). *Exports and Reexports (December)*. Hong Kong:Government Printer.
  – (1976). *Exports and Reexports (December)*. Hong Kong:Government Printer.
  – (1977). *Exports and Reexports (December)*. Hong Kong:Government Printer.
Hopkins, Keith (ed.) (1971). *Hong Kong: The Industrial Colony*. Hong Kong: Oxford University Press.
Hoselitz, B. F. (1960). 'Economic Growth in Latin America', in *First International Conference of Economic History*, Stockholm.
  – (1963). 'Main Concepts in the Analysis of the Social Implications of Technical Change', in Hoselitz and Moore (eds.), *Industrialization and Society*.
  – (1964). 'A Sociological Approach to Economic Development', in Novack and Lekackman (eds.), *Development and Society*.
Hoselitz, B. F. and Moore, W. E. (1963). *Industrialization and Society*. Paris: Mouton.
Hou, Ch'i-ming (1965). *Foreign Investment and Economic Development in China, 1840–1937*. Cambridge:Harvard University Press.
Hsü, F. L. K. and Ho, J. H. (1945). 'Guild and Kinship among the Butchers of West Town', *American Sociological Review*, 10:357.
Hubbard, G. P. (1935). *Eastern Industrialization*. New York:Oxford University Press.
Huizinga, Johan (1950). *Homo Ludens*. Boston: Beacon Press.
Hymes, D. (ed.) (1972). *Reinventing Anthropology*. New York:Random House.
Jarvie, I. C. and Agassi, J. (eds.) (1969). *Hong Kong: A Society in Transition*. London:Routledge & Kegan Paul.
Johnson, Graham (1972). 'Natives, Migrants and Voluntary Associations', unpublished Ph.D. manuscript.
Kahn, Joel (1974). 'Imperialism and the Reproduction of Capitalism: towards a definition of the Indonesian social formation', *Critique of Anthropology*, 2:1.
  – (1975). 'Economic Scale and the Cycle of Petty Commodity Production in West Sumatra', in M. Bloch (ed.), *Marxist Analyses and Social Anthropology*.
  – (1978). 'Ideology and Social Structure in Indonesia', *Comparative Studies in Society and History*, 20:103.
Kaplan, David (1968). 'The Formal-Substantive Controversy in Economic Anthropology', *Southwest Journal of Anthropology*, 24:228.
Kates, George N. (1948). *Chinese Household Furniture*. New York:Harper.
Kato, Shigesi (1936). 'On the Hong or the Association of Merchants in China

with Especial Reference to the Institution in T'ang and Sung Periods', *Memoirs of the Toyo Bunko Research Department*, 8:45.

Keller, Bonnie B. (1967). *The Woodcarvers of Zambia*. Livingstone:The National Museum of Zambia.

Keyfitz, Nathan (1959). 'The Interlocking of Social and Economic Factors in Asian Development', *The Canadian Journal of Economic and Political Science*, 25:34.

Kuznets, Simon (1963a). 'Underdeveloped Countries and the Pre-Industrial Phase in the Advanced Countries', in Agarwala and Singh (eds.), *The Economics of Underdevelopment*.

   – (1963b). 'Consumption, Industrialization and Urbanization', in Hoselitz and Moore (eds.), *Industrialization and Society*.

Kyi, Zuh-tsing (1931). 'Shanghai's Hardware Trade', *CEJ*, 8:551.

Lamson, H. D. (1931). 'The Effects of Industrialization on Village Livelihood', *CEJ*, 9:1025.

Lattimore, O. (1960). 'The Industrial Impact on China 1800–1950', in *First International Conference on Economic History*. Stockholm.

Lau, P. T. (1918). 'The Story of the Jade Industry', *Chinese Social and Political Science Review*, 3:352.

LeClair, E. E. (1962). 'Economic Theory and Economic Anthropology', *American Anthropologist*, 64:1179.

LeClair, E. E. and Schneider, H. (1968). *Economic Anthropology*. New York: Holt, Rhinehart & Winston.

Lee, P. C. (ed.) (1961–6). *Hong Kong Album*. Hong Kong:Sin Po Amalgamated.

Lee, Y. L. (1928). *Some Aspects of the Labor Situation in Canton*. Canton: Canton Y.M.C.A.

Lethbridge, Henry J. (1969). 'Hong Kong Under Japanese Occupation', in Jarvie and Agassi (eds.). *Hong Kong: A Society in Transition*.

Levy, M. J. and Shih, K. H. (1949). *The Rise of the Modern Chinese Business Class*. New York:Institute of Pacific Relations.

Lewis, W. A. (1962). 'Forward', in T. S. Epstein (ed.), *Economic Development and Social Change in South India*. Manchester:University of Manchester Press.

   – (1963). 'Economic Development with Unlimited Supplies of Labor', in Agarwala and Singh (eds.), *The Economics of Underdevelopment*.

   – (1964). 'Exporting Manufactures', in G. Meier (ed.), *Leading Issues in Economic Development*.

Liao, T'ai-ch'u (1948). 'The Apprentices in Ch'eng Tu During and After the War', *Yenching Journal of Social Studies*, 4:89.

Lieu, D. K. (1927). *China's Industries and Finance*. Peking: Shao Chang Press.

   – (1936). *The Growth and Industrialization of Shanghai*. Shanghai: Institute of Pacific Relations.

Lin, Yüeh-hwa (1947). *The Golden Wing*. New York:Columbia University Press.

Lo, Hsiang-lin (1963). *Hong Kong and its External Communications Before 1842*. Hong Kong:Institute of Chinese Culture.

Lo, Kuan-chung (1970). *The Romance of the Three Kingdoms*. Hong Kong: Kelley & Walsh.

Lockwood, E. H. (1927). 'Labor Unions in Canton', *Chinese Recorder* (July).

Lowe, Chuan-hwa (1932). *Facing Labor Issues in China*. Shanghai: Institute of Pacific Relations.

Luff, John (1967). 'The Hidden Years'. Hong Kong:*South China Morning Post*.

Bibliography

MacGowan, D. J. (1888–9). 'Chinese Guilds or Chambers of Commerce and Trade Unions', *Journal of the Royal Asiatic Society North China Branch*, 21:133.

Malinowski, Bronislaw (1961). 'Introduction' in B. Malinowski, *Argonauts of the Western Pacific*. Prospect Heights, IL: Waveland Press, Inc. (reissued 1984).

Malraux, Andre (1934). *Man's Fate*. New York:Modern Library.

Mao, Tse-tung (1967). *The Selected Works of Mao Tse-tung*. Peking:Foreign Languages Press.

Marglin, Stephen A. (1974). 'What Do Bosses Do?', *The Review of Radical Political Economists*, 6:60.

Marx, Karl (1939). *Grundrisse, Foundations of the Critique of Political Economy*. London:Pelican Marx Library (1973).

– (1965). *Pre-Capitalist Economic Formations*. New York:International Publishers.

– (1967). *Capital*. New York:International Publishers.

Mauss, Marcel (1951). *The Gift*. Glencoe:Free Press.

McCormick, T. J. (1967). *The China Market*. Chicago:Quadrangle Books.

Meier, Gerald (1964). *Leading Issues in Development Economics*. New York: Oxford University Press.

Meillasoux, C. (1972). 'From Reproduction to Production: a Marxist Approach to Economic Anthropology', *Economy and Society*, 1:93.

Mermelstein, David (ed.) (1970). *Economics: Mainstream Readings and Radical Critiques*. New York:Random House.

Minkes, A. L. (1952–3). 'A Note on Handicrafts in Underdeveloped Areas', *Economic Development and Cultural Change*, 1:156.

Moore, W. E. (1948). 'Primitives and Peasants in Industry', *Social Research*, 15:44.

– (1963). 'Industrialization and Society', in Hoselitz and Moore (eds.), *Industrialization and Society*.

Morse, H. B. (1909). *The Gilds of China*. London:Longman, Green & Co.

Moulder, F. W. (1977). *Japan, China and the Modern World Economy*. Cambridge:Cambridge University Press.

Murphey, Rhoads (1962). 'The City as a Center of Change: Western Europe and China', in Wagner and Mikesell (eds.), *Readings in Cultural Geography*. Chicago: University of Chicago Press.

– (1970). *Treaty Ports and China's Modernization, What Went Wrong*, Michigan Papers in Chinese Studies No. 7.

Myers, R. H. (1970). *The Chinese Peasant Economy, 1890–1949*. Cambridge: Harvard University Press.

– (1972). 'The Commercialization of Agriculture in Modern China', in Wilmott (ed.), *Economic Organization in Chinese Society*.

Myint, H. (1963). 'An Interpretation of Economic Backwardness', in Agarwala and Singh (eds.), *The Economics of Underdevelopment*.

Nagano, Akira (1931). *The Development of Capitalism in China*. Tokyo:Institute of Pacific Relations.

Nathan, Andrew (1972). 'Imperialism's Effects on China', *Bulletin of Concerned Asian Scholars*, 4:3.

Nieh, C. L. (1933). *China's Industrial Development: Its Problems and Prospects*. Banff:Institute of Pacific Relations.

Novack, D. and Lekackman, R. (1964). *Development and Society*. New York: St Martin's Press.

Bibliography

Nurkse, Ragnar (1964). 'The Size of the Market and the Inducement to Invest', in Novack and Lekackman (eds.), *Development and Society*.

Odets, Clifford (1935). *Waiting for Lefty*. New York:Modern Library.

O'Laughlin, Bridget (1975). 'Marxist Approaches in Anthropology', in Siegel, Beals and Tyler (eds.), *Annual Review of Anthropology*.

Olsen, Stephen M. (1972). 'The Inculcation of Economic Values in Taipei Business Families', in W. E. Wilmott (ed.), *Economic Organization in Chinese Society*.

Orans, M. (1966). 'Surplus', *Human Organization*, 25:24.

Owen, N. (1971). 'Economic Policy', in K. Hopkins (ed.) *Hong Kong: The Industrial Colony*.

Pearson, Harry W. (1957). 'The Economy Has No Surplus: Critique of a theory of development', in Polanyi *et al.* (eds.), *Trade and Market in the Early Empires*.

P'eng, Tse-yi (1957). *Historical Materials on Modern Chinese Handicrafts* (in Chinese). Peking.

— (1965). The Reconstruction and Functions of Handicraft and Mercantile Associations in Late 19th Century Chinese Cities (in Chinese). Li Shih Yen Chiu.

Phelps-Brown, E. H. (1971). 'The Hong Kong Economy: Achievements and Prospects', in K. Hopkins (ed.), *Hong Kong: The Industrial Colony*.

Pillsbury, Barbara (1975). Review of Wilmott (ed.), *Economic Organization in Chinese Society*, *American Anthropologist*, 77:392.

Polanyi, Karl (1944). *The Great Transformation*. Boston:Beacon Press.

Polanyi, Karl *et al.* (1957). *Trade and Market in the Early Empires*. Glencoe: Free Press.

— (1968). *Primitive, Archaic and Modern Economies*. New York: Doubleday.

Potter, Jack (1968). *Capitalism and the Chinese Peasant*. Berkeley:University of California Press.

Rankin, Mary B. (1971). *Early Chinese Revolutionaries, Radical Intellectuals in Shanghai and Chekiang*. Cambridge:Harvard University Press.

Rear, John (1971a). 'One Brand of Politics', in K. Hopkins (ed.) *Hong Kong: The Industrial Colony*.

— (1971b). 'The Law of the Constitution', in K. Hopkins (ed.), *Hong Kong: the Industrial Colony*.

Redfield, Robert (1960). *The Little Community/Peasant Society and Culture*. Chicago:University of Chicago Press.

Robushka, Albert (1973). 'Towards 1997', serialized article in the *Hong Kong Standard*, August 12, 19 and 26.

Roseberry, William (1976). 'Peasants and Primitive Accumulation: Western Europe and Venezuela compared', unpublished paper prepared for symposium at American Anthropological Association meetings, 1976.

Rottenberg, Simon (1952–3). Labor Relations in an Underdeveloped Economy', *Economic Development and Cultural Change*, 1:250.

Ruscoe, Nigei (1963). *Hong Kong Register*, Hong Kong: Far Eastern Economic Review.

Sahlins, Marshall (1960). 'Political Power and Economy in Primitive Society', in Dole and Carneiro (eds.), *Essays in the Science of Culture*. New York: Crowell.

— (1965). 'On the Sociology of Primitive Exchange', in M. Banton (ed.),

Bibliography

Relevance of Models for Social Anthropology. A.S.A. Monograph No. 1. London:Tavistock.
- (1969). Economic Anthropology and Anthropological Economics. *Social Science Information* 8.
- (1972). *Stone Age Economics*. Chicago:Aldine.
Salaff, Janet (1974). '"Modern Times" in Hong Kong', *Bulletin of Concerned Asian Scholars*, 6:2.
Salisbury, R. F. (1968). 'Anthropology and Economics', in O. von Mering (ed.), *Anthropology and Related Disciplines*. Pittsburgh:University of Pittsburgh Press.
Shiba, Yoshinobu (1977). 'Ningpo and its Hinterland', in G. W. Skinner (ed.), *The City in Late Imperial China*. Stanford:Stanford University Press.
Shih, Kuo-heng (1944). *China Enters the Machine Age*. Cambridge:Harvard University Press.
Sillin, Robert (1972). 'Marketing and Credit in a Hong Kong Wholesale Market', in W. E. Wilmott (ed.), *Economic Organization in Chinese Society*.
Sjoberg, Gideon (1960). *The Pre-Industrial City*. New York:Free Press.
Skinner, G. W. (1964—5). 'Marketing and Social Structure in Rural China', *Journal of Asian Studies*, 24:3, 195, 363.
- (1977). *The City in Late Imperial China*. Stanford:Stanford University Press.
Smedley, A. (1974). *The Great Road*. New York:Monthly Review Press.
Smelser, Neil J. (1963). 'Mechanism of Change and Adjustment to Change', in Hoselitz and Moore (eds.), *Industrialization and Society*.
Smith, Henry (1966). *John Stuart Mill's Other Island: A Study of Economic Development in Hong Kong*. London:Institute of Economic Affairs.
Sowerby, Arthur de C. (1926). 'A New Art-craft in Shanghai', *The China Journal of Science and Arts*, 8:1.
Spengler, J. J. (1956—7). 'Cottage Industries: A Comment', *Economic Development and Cultural Change*, 5:371.
Stanley, Arthur (1914). 'Chinese Woodcarving', *Journal of the Royal Asiatic Society North China Branch*, 45:76.
Steward, Julian (1955). *Theory of Culture Change*. Urbana:University of Illinois Press.
Suttles, Gerald D. (1968). *The Social Order of the Slum*. Chicago:University of Chicago Press.
Sweezey, Paul (1942). *The Theory of Capitalist Development*. New York: Monthly Review Press.
Szepanik, Edward (1958). *The Economic Growth of Hong Kong*. London: Oxford University Press.
Ta Kung Pao (1967). *We Shall Win*. Hong Kong:Ta Kung Pao.
Tao, L. K. (1929). 'Handicraft Workers of Peking', *Chinese Social and Political Science Review*, 13:1.
Tauber, Irene (1963). 'Hong Kong: Migrants and Metropolis', *Population Index*, 29:3.
Tawney, R. H. (1932). *Land and Labor in China*. London: George Allen & Unwin.
Tayler, J. B. (1928). *Farm and Factory in China*. London:Student Christian Movement.
- (1930). 'The Hopei Pottery Industry and the Problem of Modernization', *Chinese Social and Political Science Review*, 14:184.

146

Bibliography

Terray, Emmanuel (1972). *Marxism and Primitive Society*. New York:Monthly Review Press.

Topley, Marjorie (1969). *Anthropology and Sociology in Hong Kong*. Hong Kong:University of Hong Kong Press.

Udy, Stanley (1959). *Organization of Work: a comparative analysis of production among pre-industrial peoples*. New Haven:H.R.A.F. Press.

Van der Sprenkle, Sybille (1962). *Legal Institutions of Manchu China*. London: Athlone.

Wallerstein, I. (1974). *The Modern World System: capitalist origins of the European world economy in the sixteenth century*. New York:Academic Press.

Wang, Kuo-sieu (1929). 'Chinese Influence on English Decorative Art in the 18th Century', *Chinese Social and Political Science Review*, 13:405.

Ward, Barbara (1972). 'A Small Factory in Hong Kong, Some Aspects of its Internal Organization', in W. E. Wilmott (ed.), *Economic Organization in Chinese Society*.

Watson, J. L. (1974). 'Restaurants and Remittances: Chinese Emigrant Workers in London', in Foster and Kemper (eds.), *Anthropologists in Cities*. Boston: Little, Brown & Co.

Wheelwright, E. L. and MacFarlane, B. (1970). *The Chinese Road to Socialism*. New York:Monthly Review Press.

White, Leslie (1949). *The Science of Culture*. New York:Grove Press.

Wilmott, W. E. (ed.) (1972). *Economic Organization in Chinese Society*. Stanford:Stanford University Press.

Wittfogel, Karl (1957). *Oriental Despotism*. New Haven:Yale University Press.

Wong Po-shang (1958). *The Influx of Chinese Capital into Hong Kong Since 1937*. Hong Kong:Kai Ming Press.

Woo, Sing-lim (ed.) (1937). *Prominent Chinese of Hong Kong*. Hong Kong: Five Continents Book Co.

Wright, S. and Cartwright, C. W. (1908). *Twentieth Century Impressions of Hong Kong, Macau, Shanghai, etc.* London:the authors.

INDEX

accumulation, 16, 47, 52
  of capital, 13, 21, 74, 109, 125, 129
  primitive, 7, 133, 135
alienation, 8, 19
  from the means of production, 66
  of workers from the tools of their trade, 75, 78, 86
anthropology
  Marxist approaches in, 2
anti-British sentiment, 76
apprentice(s), 7–10, 15, 23–33, 44, 47, 49, 50, 55–7, 60, 62, 119, 128
  beating of, 26, 27
  carpenter's, 31, 33
  carver's, 27–31
  labor, 25, 31, 32, 107
apprenticeship, 9, 21, 23–6, 28, 32, 65, 97, 103, 119, 131
  contract, 23–5
  ordeal, 23
  period/term, 24, 26, 28, 32, 33, 57
art-carved furniture, 1, 8, 23, 34, 56, 59, 92
  decline in quality of Hong Kong made, 19, 107
  industry, 6, 10, 16, 19, 21, 26, 30, 32, 34, 46, 53–6, 59–62, 68, 70, 72–4, 76, 77, 79, 84, 86, 87, 89–91, 94, 95, 100–2, 109–11, 116, 120, 124, 126, 128–31, 133, 134; interrelatedness of factories and shops in, 100
  production, 26, 75, 78, 123; constraints of international competition on, 92–3; success factors in, 106–7; supplies of wood for, 92; synthetic structure of, 51, 75
artisan, 31, 40, 71, 106, 121, 125, 129
Artistic Woodworkers' Union, 69, 71, 75

Babbage principle, 6
bonus
  New Years, 46

boss–worker relations, 40, 43, 47, 78, 106, 131
  closeness of, 43, 78
  commercialization of, 52
bourgeoisie, 68, 93, 94
  compradore, 84
  international, 94
  national, 84, 134
  native, 94
business
  abstract skills of modern, 124
  expenses, 10, 103, 104
  practices, 10, 21, 90, 95, 105
  relations, 98, 101

camphorwood, 16, 37, 38, 55, 59, 68, 69, 109, 110
  chests, 1, 16, 18, 19, 23, 34, 39, 53, 67, 99, 109, 127
Camphorwood Chest Workers' Guild, 68, 72
Camphorwood Trunk Workers' Union, 69, 71, 72, 74, 75, 80
Canton, 10, 11, 13, 36, 53, 55, 67, 71, 90, 91, 109
Cantonese, 12, 53–7, 69, 79, 80, 98, 110
capital, 16, 18, 20, 23, 30, 32–4, 40–2, 55, 68, 73, 74, 90, 91, 93, 95, 107–10, 113, 118, 124, 130, 131, 134
  as a social relation, 6
  availability of, 106, 107
  concentration of, 18, 78, 86, 88, 107, 125
  equipment, 48
  intensiveness, 18, 107
  requirements of carved-furniture production, 19, 35, 41, 42, 51, 52, 75, 106
capitalism, 5, 6, 133
  central, 133; pattern of transition to, 133
  industrial, 23, 132

Index

peripheral, 133
capitalist, 2, 6, 52, 84, 91, 124, 129, 132, 134, 135
   class, 90, 131, 132
   mode of production, 17, 130, 133, 134; all leveling rationality of the, 129, 135; evolution of the, 1
   production, 7
   social formation, 90
carpenter(s), 11–13, 16–18, 20, 26, 30–5, 42, 47–51, 53, 56, 62, 68, 73, 75, 76, 85, 89, 104, 129
carpenter's union, 68
carpentry, 19, 27, 30–2, 38, 41, 48, 107, 123, 125
   stage of production, 17, 18
carved-furniture industry, 1, 8, 12, 40, 43
carved-wood furniture industry, 12
carved-wood products, 13, 15, 19, 36, 57
   market for, 18, 92, 109
carver(s), 12, 13, 16, 17, 19, 20, 26, 28, 30, 31, 34–6, 38, 40–2, 47–51, 53, 55, 57, 60–2, 68, 69, 75, 76, 85, 89, 125–9
   rough, 13, 27, 35–40, 49
   rural temple, 11, 35, 126
   skills: cheapening of, 125
   smooth, 13, 27, 35–7, 39, 40, 49, 51
carver's union, 17, 20, 69
carving(s), 11, 12, 19, 31, 38, 40, 55, 59–61, 126, 128, 133
   temple, 11, 57, 59
   wood, 8, 10, 35, 37, 57, 59, 60, 67, 121; black market in, 127; factories, 8; industry, 55, 67
Chinese Communist government, 17, 54
Chinese Communist party, 17, 67
Chippendale, Sir Thomas, 10–11
Chun Wah Union, 67, 70
class(es)
   conflict, 131
   consciousness, 78; national consciousness as opposed to, 84
   interests, 84, 130
   polarization of, 130, 131
   solidarity, 61
   struggle, 131
   working, 84, 131
commercial relations, 21, 90, 95, 99
communist
   China, 13, 77, 84, 88
   ideology, 61, 82
   union, 17, 69, 70, 74, 120, 127
community, 66
   occupational, 62

craft
   parochialism, 17, 21, 52, 68, 88, 130
   practitioners, 35, 52, 68
   production, 1, 25, 35, 94, 129–31; evolution of, 129; traditional structure of, 88
craftsman(men), 5, 6, 12, 23, 28, 67, 126
   master, 24
   relation to his work, 21
credit, 46, 47, 101
   worker, 45
   lines of, 102

debt, 65, 102, 103
   and labor mobility, 65–6
   level of, 46
   relationship, 46
deferred payments, 102
deliveries, 27, 102
detail laborers, 6, 37
diversification, 18, 48, 108, 118, 125, 131
   market, 21
division of labor, 1, 6, 7, 18, 20, 27, 30, 34, 36, 37, 41, 106, 129, 130, 132
   carving slots in, 27, 37
   elaboration of, 5, 6, 8, 31, 35, 37, 125
   manufacturing, 17, 30, 31, 34, 51, 131, 133
   niches in the, 27, 38, 52
Dongyang county, Zhejiang, 12, 54, 56-60, 96, 98, 104, 125-7
   same native place association, 60, 61, 69, 98, 117

economic base, 2, 3, 4
economic development, 105
   disjointed character of, 5
exploitation, 47, 48
export(s), 18, 53, 57, 60, 90, 99, 117
   of Hong Kong made wooden furniture, 16, 19
   from the People's Republic of China, 19, 60, 93

forces of production, 2, 7, 37
   cyclical movement of, 132

gambling, 43–6, 72, 127
   debts, 41, 45
Guangdong, 53, 86, 109
guarantor, 23–5
guild(s), 21, 23, 25, 32, 67, 68, 70–3, 79, 82, 109, 116, 118–20, 130
   and castes, 23

149

Index

Index

Index

Index

DATE DUE